PASS THE POVERTY PLEASE

by

PATTY NEWMAN

in collaboration with

JOYCE WENGER

CONSTRUCTIVE ACTION, Inc.
P.O. Box 4006
Whittier, California 90607

PASS THE POVERTY PLEASE

© 1966 by Constructive Action, Inc.

CONSTRUCTIVE ACTION, Inc.
P.O. Box 4006
Whittier, California 90607

Printed in the United States of America

TABLE OF CONTENTS

Chapter One

THE GREATEST "SNOW" ON EARTH

"THE WAR ON POVERTY," said Senator Gordon Allott, "has been heralded in a fashion that would make P. T. Barnum's heart leap for joy, were he still alive. The advance publicity men and the barkers have been diligently plying their trade. The atmosphere has definitely been 'circus,' and after reading the bill, perhaps a circus setting is appropriate after all. With the enactment of this hastily drafted, ill-considered legislation the world renowned Ringling Bros. and Barnum & Bailey Circus will be relegated to the 'Second Greatest Show on Earth.'" [1]

The greatest show on earth! The curtain has risen on a federal show the like of which you've never seen. Your tax money is being used to tell the poor how badly they are being treated, how they must organize and "demand" that which everyone else has, and how they needn't worry if they get thrown in jail in the process because tax money will be used to get them out and to hire lawyers in their defense. School boycotts, rent strikes, and demonstrations (plus baby-sitting costs while all of this is going on) are being financed with tax dollars. Taxpayers are paying for the poor to go to expensive theaters, to have dinners in fine restaurants, to at long last live as the "other half" lives—all with no worries about paying for it. And if enough poor can not be found to participate, high-salaried "directors" are hired to go out and find them!

Some of these bureau-of-the-missing-poor directors found families who said there wasn't enough heat in their apartment during the cold spell this past January in New York. As a result more than 37 of these poor have been enjoying all the services of the elegant Hotel Astor (plus $9 per day per person for meals) for over a month now and they're still there! [2] In three-room suites and with no drudgery of housework (their beds are made by the chambermaids) who can blame them for thinking this War on Poverty is really great . . . and it isn't costing them a thing! The hotel maids, clerks, and the like are a bit critical, though. It seems the new guests are a bit stingy with tips, despite the suite charity.

Perhaps this whole program is meant as "kindness," but after more than a year and a half of concentrated study and investigation, we have our doubts. But regardless of the real motivation behind the anti-poverty show, we agree with Al Capp who, in a recent Little Abner show, asked, "How can Daisy Mae be made a widow without physical violence?" The cartoon computer answered, "You . . . can . . . kill . . . with . . . kindness." [3]

Just what is this multi-billion-dollar spectacular called the Economic Opportunity Act? Don't expect a simple answer.

The Act itself is divided into seven titles. Some of them expound the capability of privately organized councils (similar to the "communes" of Communist China) to assume the functions of locally elected government, and each of them offers a fat bone of taxpayers' money to be fought over with fanatical fury.

It is impossible to outline this law neatly with everything in the proper place. Because of overlapping authority, too much authority or no authority at all, vague and confused definitions, and lack of any clear-cut line of procedure, the administration of this poverty program is a chaotic shambles. The result is that anyone foolish enough to attempt to figure it out is risking candidacy for the mayor of insanityland.

Despite charges and evidence of graft, patronage, and political blackmail, the present rubber stamp Congress continues to fill the poverty platter with tempting goodies. Congress refused to accept a single Congressional amendment that might have at least helped to correct some of the glaring ills of the law. Outvoted in every attempt, the opposition went back to its corner to lick its wounds and wait—wait for a bemused and seemingly unconcerned public to wake up and help.

Until help arrives, Congressional opposition must look on, helplessly, as the heavily armored anti-poverty political tanks move ahead, crushing the hopes of decent citizens for improvement of the American way of life. There has been an unbroken string of exposures of waste and fraud, but the anti-poverty generals merely swat at the irritating flies and make minor adjustments. Their philosophy remains unchanged: "Sticks and stones may break our bones, but words will never stop us."

In keeping with the wordsmanship which has

become the obsession of politicians, the Economic Opportunity Act has been dubbed, "The War on Poverty." Now one of the first requisites of any well run war is to know your enemy, and since, in this case, the enemy has been proclaimed "poverty," let's identify it. For you readers who are thinking, "Who has to acquaint me with poverty . . . I know all I want to know about poverty," please, stay with us. You might find that your brand of poverty is quite outdated in this updated war.

Saul Alinsky (more about him later) defines poverty simply as not having any money. Such a basic definition is, of course, completely unacceptable to the sophisticated types who have much more in mind than feeding the hungry. What specific amount of income is considered sufficient to provide the necessities of life in the prosperous United States? Should it be $1,000? $3,000? $5,000? Never mind about the size of the family, where they live, what their non-money income is, how many televisions or late model cars they own. Pick a figure, runs the formula, then write and pass a law.

Armed with sociological reasoning for ammunition, it was arbitrarily decided that any family living on an income of less than $3,000 a year was living in "abject poverty" and any family living on less than $5,000 was "deprived." [4] Now those of us who have successfully struggled to make ends meet on $5,000 a year can relax and accept our "deprived" station in life as society's responsibility, not ours.

By next year a $5,000 or $6,000 or $8,000 bracket could be considered "poverty," and just think how many more dependents that would put into the protecting and supporting arms of the federal government. And don't forget about the old switcheroo of "cultural poverty," which has nothing to do with income. All those deemed "culturally" deprived can also be computed in the poverty percentage, thus qualifying the area for federal help by way of *your* taxes.

The use of the government's statistical approach to determine poverty means, simply, that as long as there is a substantial difference in incomes there will always be people who may be considered poverty-stricken. Thus, the happy warriors will always be assured of "have nots" to be helped by taking from the "haves."

When we decide to "take from the haves and give to the have nots" as President Johnson said,* then we have basically agreed to share the wealth. There is no gentle way to say that this is anything but acceptance of the leveling concept of socialism and communism. Undoubtedly what begins with sharing the wealth will end with sharing the poverty.

And next will come the bit about a "minimum income" for everyone. Congressman James H. Scheuer is chairman of a group of some 150 liberal Democrats in Congress called the "Democratic Study Committee." This group, in a report on January 6, 1966, urged that the government "begin to provide a minimum income for everyone." [5] This was to be accomplished, in part, by a "negative tax on income," which would provide that a poor person or family, instead of paying a tax to the government, would get a payment from the government to assure at least a minimum living. The group did not comment on what would happen when a poor family "blew" the whole mini-

* "We are going to take all of the money that we think is unnecessarily being spent and take it from the 'haves' and give it to the 'have nots' that need it so much." President Lyndon B. Johnson launched the Great Society with these words in a White House speech, January 15, 1964.

mum income in the first month . . . or perhaps the group had in mind *controlling the spending* as well as the giving.

While the Statue of Liberty says with silent lips, "Give me your poor," we are; handing out more than $50 BILLION a year to our "poor."[6] Our government's relief bill is increasing at a much higher rate than the population increase. Private industry is spending a fortune on its own war on poverty in training and re-training programs. Combining government, industry, and private welfare programs, over $100 BILLION (an amount almost equal to our national budget) is being spent each year in a war on poverty.[7]

If this governmental war on poverty does nothing else, it certainly helps to prove that "It Pays to be Poor," which may be some sort of consolation prize for the about-to-be-poor taxpayer.

The average family earning it and qualifying for poverty aid, according to a most interesting and statistically documented article in the November 1, 1965, U.S. News and World Report.

Such a family, according to the report, would have no Income or Social Security taxes to pay, and would reap all the benefits from the ever-growing list of aids-to-the-poor which it couldn't possibly afford on $5,000 a year. Besides a basic relief check or an Aid-to-Families-with-Dependent-Children (AFDC) check, benefits include food stamps, rent subsidies, free medical and dental care, free nursery school, free remedial education, psychiatric consultation, speech therapy, anti-poverty jobs, free trips to theaters and other places of entertainment, family camping trips . . . the list goes on and on and on. It's all free, and there has been a concentrated effort that no stigma of "handout or charity" be attached to this "handout and charity."

These it seems, are the "rights" of an "abused and excluded" sector of society. Add up all these benefits in dollars and cents and it is easy to see why working for an income of $5,000 is just plain foolish.

All of this has been bitterly labeled as "relief socialism" and a new kind of "slavery" for the Negro by a prominent young Negro woman. Myrna Bain, who is one of the founders of a new Negro magazine called *Advance* (Newark, N.J.), recently wrote an article which columnist John Chamberlain described as "an entirely unorthodox discussion of socialism." Miss Bain wrote:

"To the extent that a slave, any slave, is not free to do as he or she pleases with her life and property, to the extent that the old slave masters provided food, shelter and burial for their chattels, to the extent that all slaves were treated equally as slaves (whether in the house or field), to that extent slavery approximates and carries out 'the cradle to grave' protection and 'equal distribution' of wealth and property that is inherent in all Socialist doctrine.

"The current anti-poverty program plus its previous predecessors such as the WPA, CCC, and aid to dependent children, has all too much in common with the old system of paternalistic slavery." [8]

To any thinking person the War on Poverty equals paternalistic slavery. To some that's bad, but to others that's the means to the power for which they hunger.

After determining just exactly *what* poverty is, the warriors had to determine *where* it was. This, of course, was no problem.

It was quickly discovered that the most poverty was wherever the most voters were.

Pockets of poverty, fringes of poverty, and culturally deprived groups were easily discovered in almost all *concentrated* areas. When West Virginia wondered why its anti-poverty allotment had been only around $400,000 and the high-income (and populous) State of New Jersey had received over $12.5 million,9 it was explained that dispersed poverty was difficult to deal with effectively!

Farms account for over half of our nation's "poor" and yet only 5-10% of the Community Action money goes "way out thar."10 Obviously there are "extenuating circumstances" in all of the pages of like examples that we have collected. Vote buying has nothing to do with it?

More poverty funds will undoubtedly be spent in Los Angeles than in any other county in the nation. You're wrong if you think Los Angeles has more poverty than any other county . . . but can you name any county that contains more Congressional districts?

Now that we know what poverty is and where it is, we must look at the battle plan. Actually, the Economic Opportunity Act can best be explained by saying it is unexplainable.

However, if one boils down the cabalistic phraseology, here's the way this $1.9 BILLION law looks: 11

TITLE I

THE JOB CORPS: Unemployed and out-of-school poverty youths are sent to live in rural camps or urban centers and are to be exposed to remedial education, vocational training, and the finer things in life.

NEIGHBORHOOD YOUTH CORPS: Poverty youths are employed by their home community agencies with wages paid by the federal government.

COLLEGE WORK-STUDY: On campus and off campus jobs for college students from poverty homes. Wages are paid for by the federal government.

TITLE II

COMMUNITY ACTION PROGRAMS: This wide open door allows almost any group to devise almost any kind of program for people whose income, supposedly, is less than $3,000. With the vague understanding that these programs will help cure the causes of poverty, the federal government divvies up 90% of the cost.

ADULT BASIC EDUCATION: A state educational agency can initiate programs for people whose inability to read and write the English language constitutes a handicap. No age or income requirements needed to qualify.

TITLE III

RURAL LOANS AND COOPERATIVE FARM PLANS: This section was initially so extreme in its collectivist concept that comparatively little activity so far has been noted.

TITLE IV

LOANS TO SMALL BUSINESS: A program aimed at catching the poorest of poor credit risks. Repayment is fully guaranteed by the federal government for loans on marginal businesses given to applicants who have failed to get a loan approved from any other source.

LOANS TO PRIVATE BUSINESS: Loans under this section are to be used to hire the long term unemployed and low income families.

TITLE V

WORK EXPERIENCE PROGRAMS: A Neighborhood Youth Corps program for adults aimed at giving training benefits ($) to unemployed heads of families who are on welfare. This is affectionately known as the "Happy Pappy" program.

EXPERIMENTAL, PILOT, AND DEMONSTRATION PROJECTS: You name it!

TITLE VI

ADMINISTRATION: Sets up the Office of Economic Opportunity and gives to its director-boss practically unlimited powers.

VISTA: This is the code name for Volunteers in Service to America and is the War on Poverty's version of a domestic Peace Corps.

TITLE VII

This title simply provides that most of the money received by the poor under Titles I and II shall not be considered as income for purposes of qualifying for welfare!

* * * * * * * * * * *

By the end of the ensuing pages you probably will be able to guess some of the why's and wherefors of what is going on in this poverty war. Of one thing we are quite sure . . . you will be much more keenly attuned to the popular principle of letting the government give what you have to those who haven't what you have.

There being no un-confused manner in which to approach the Economic Opportunity Act's War on Poverty, we will proceed like the man in the Office of Economic Opportunity who decided to chart the funding sources and lines of authority of each title of the law. After drawing lines and cross-lines in so many directions that one line could not be distinguished from the other, he threw up his hands in disgust and said, "What the hell. Full steam ahead."

Chapter Two

CAST OF CHARACTERS

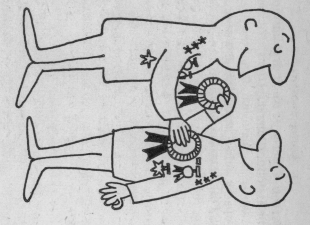

Any good soldier can tell you it helps to have some knowledge of your generals, and this particular war has some downright fascinating top brass.

ADAM CLAYTON POWELL, the Paris-loving nepotist and delinquent Member of Congress, pinned five stars on his own shoulders with the words:

"I control all labor legislation . . . all education legislation, the man-power training and redevelopment program, vocational rehabilitation, and, of greater importance today, the

War on Poverty. This is legislative power. This is political power." [1]

The wacky thing about this typically modest appraisal of his power is that it comes very close to being the truth. As chairman of the powerful House Committee on Education and Labor, he controls the purse strings of the War on Poverty, and that is a powerful enough weapon to justify a brass hat and a few stars in any man's war.

Mr. Powell runs his House committee with an iron hand. At his whim he initiates anti-poverty "hearings," listens to his choice of witnesses, and then arbitrarily cuts off any further testimony.[2] He will obtain money for all sorts of travel expenses for his investigating "task forces," but has been known to conveniently overlook the need for money to provide a stenographer, so that no records of any worth result from all the expensive investigating.[3]

The most recent War on Poverty "investigation" was given $230,000 of tax money for a highly publicized six-month "in depth" probe of the "war" across the nation.[4] Yet the only thing accomplished so far is a masterful detective plot involving, not the War on Poverty, but who-did-what-with-how-much-money. It is embarrassingly apparent that so far Powell's investigating subcommittee has not filed monthly progress reports (required by House rules), has not submitted monthly financial statements (required by House rules), and has not reported their projected plans for each following month (required by House rules).[5]

Ignoring laws and rules with which he does not agree is a habit with Mr. Powell. He tells his Harlem congregation—he's a minister too—that they do not have to obey laws which they had no part in making.[6] As for his investigating task force, they are not talking except to say they need more money. Only $17,000 of the $230,000 is left.

When Adam Clayton Powell feels anti-poverty battle plans are not progressing quite to his way of planning, he lashes out in bitter criticism of someone, almost anyone, declaring the whole program to be filled with "giant fiestas of political patronage."[7] This is true only until he gets what he wants, then everything is peaches and cream. Getting what he wants is usually achieved by discreet letters from pen-pal Sargent Shriver, director and top general of the war, assuring paymaster Powell that misunderstandings will be immediately straightened out . . . to Powell's satisfaction.[8] Certain members of Congress jokingly (ha-ha) refer to this as "legislation by personal letter."[9]

A New York State Supreme Court Justice expressed his opinion of Powell when he imposed a $575,000 judgment against him. Justice Maurice Wahl said, "He's like a mackerel . . . he shines, but he smells to high heaven."[10]

Adam Clayton Powell projects his love-myself-and-watch-out-if-you-don't-love-me-too control into House floor debates. He might allow an opposition bill emanating from his committee 15 or 20 minutes for presentation, but then again he can—and sometimes does—see that only 3 minutes are granted. You know, it could get downright frustrating to be a Republican under Powell, especially now that he's almost always around. His fun-filled junkets, apparently, have been relegated to second place for the War on Poverty. His attendance record during poverty hearings is near-perfect, which ought to be a sign of something or other. His intense interest is further substantiated by his statement that to make the attack a "war," not just a "skirmish," the federal government must triple its financial commitment.[11]

Mr. Powell stands firmly committed to the poor having full control over these programs. He is convinced that all War on Poverty funds must be channeled through "community groups" of the poor. He is critical of any anti-poverty agency which has any ties to, or can be outvoted by, "City Hall." Powell tends to see "City Hall" as a threat to his dictatorial powers in Harlem and elsewhere. He has long been critical of Sargent Shriver recognizing agencies that are dominated by a city's public officials (local representative government). Late in August he said, "We left it to the discretion of the director to determine the criteria for eligible organizations instead of writing it into the bill. We'll take care of that next year." [12]

This, then, may be the pattern: Powell, allied with anti-city hall militants in Chicago, Cleveland, Los Angeles, New York and elsewhere, attempting to take over not only the poverty program but effective political control as well.

SARGEANT SHRIVER, as one of the nation's most glib salesmen, is the ranking general in the War on Poverty. The rank was enhanced, not diminished, by the fact that he was also the top general of the Peace Corps, which he ran with his left hand. Or was it the other way around? Coping with just one of these programs would have been enough to exhaust the average man, but Sargent Shriver has proven himself neither average nor exhaustable. However in January 1966, according to Columnist George Jordan, "L.B.J. escalated the War on Poverty . . . he told Sargent Shriver to run it with both hands." [13] Now the Peace Corps will have to survive Shriver-less.

When Sargent Shriver was told to fire off the War on Poverty, one of his first actions was to call in Michael Harrington, whose book, "The Other America," had helped inspire the whole campaign. Mr. Shriver and Mr. Harrington had lunch together and got so carried away with plans for abolishing poverty they all but forgot to go home for two weeks.[14]

Let's take just a minute to comment on Michael Harrington. He is a self-admitted socialist, "to the left of Norman Thomas," as he puts it.[15] (Norman Thomas was, of course, the Socialist Party candidate for United States President six times.) In 1964, Harrington was Chairman of the Board of the League for Industrial Democracy which has worked for years to destroy the free enterprise system.[16] He has worked on a national effort for some years to abolish the House Committee on Un-American Activities.[17] In a speech at the University of Southern California in 1965 he said that the only question is "how" we are going to be "socialized" or "collectivized." [18] We won't dwell on Harrington, but isn't it interesting that Sargent Shriver would choose to consult with an avowed enemy of the system which made America so great?

During these two weeks of conferences Mr. Harrington solved the problem of how war could be declared on poverty when so few in this country know what *real* poverty is. Even the poor of Harlan County, Kentucky, have their own automobiles, their own television sets, and their own washing machines. This capitalistic achievement could have proved to be quite a stumbling block for an ordinary genius. But Mr. Harrington solved it very neatly by explaining that the reason American poverty "is hidden today in a way that it never was before," why it is so "socially invisible to the rest of us," is apparently because automobiles, television sets, and washing machines *are* poverty.[19]

And this was good enough logic for Sargent Shriver to hire this socialist, so scornful of the free enterprise system, as a consultant in the War on Poverty.[20]

An office to run the war had to be set up and poverty commander Shriver, being a far better promoter than administrator, has managed to set up an Office of Economic Opportunity which Ted Lewis in the New York Daily News describes as "a bureaucratic mess . . . easily the worst-run agency in Washington, which is saying a lot." [21]

The organization is so top-heavy with swivel-chair commandos that the ratio is one "brass" to every 18 Pfc's. When one considers that in Shriver's army-headquarters a private first class makes up to $19,000 a year, while the top brass *start* at $19,000, the 1-18 ratio becomes downright shocking. It becomes even more shocking when it is noted that in the Defense Department (never noted for stringent economy) the ratio is 1 to 1000.[22]

The list of full time consultants for the Office of Economic Opportunity runs to almost five pages in the Congressional Record.[23] On this list the average *full time* consultant's pay is close to $100 per day and, according to Congressional testimony, includes names of rich society do-gooders, halfbacks on football teams, newsmen and movie stars.[24] If you are ever curious about the great press relations Sargent Shriver appears to maintain, consider the number of key newsmen serving as paid "consultants."* After reviewing the con-

---

*We learned that one such consultant was Marie Ridder ($3,250) who is the wife of the bureau chief of the Ridder Publications. The Ridders have 12 dailies and 15 weeklies throughout the nation. This cleared up, at least to our satisfaction, why the Ridder publications (which control the news coverage in the San Gabriel Valley area of California) are seldom critical of any War on Poverty program.[25]

sultant list, Congressman William Ayers said, "I saw many familiar names, including some of our top Washington lobbyists and some of our top newspaper people in the United States." [26]

Despite lucrative top-level salaries, Shriver is having trouble keeping top aides on his staff. Ranking officials have been leaving the Office of Economic Opportunity as fast as Lyndon Johnson dropped Bobby Baker. Shriver attempts to cover the continuing exodus by explaining that he prefers "the best man" for a short time to a "less able man" for a continuing time. [27] But few are accepting this, even with a grain of salt. Columnist Carl T. Rowan explains that officials are resigning because they feel their authority is continuously usurped and that Shriver's aides make decisions affecting their areas which they learn about only by reading the newspapers. [28] Regardless of reasons, the problems involved are not diminishing.

When it comes to glossing over the critical evidence against the War on Poverty, Sargent Shriver truly earns his five stars. When riots and disorders erupt in various programs, they are always "unfortunate isolated incidents." When quotas are not filled, it is due only to "unrealistic goals." When Community Action programs have bogged down in a mire of political contention, Shriver cheerfully proclaims that "nobody would be yelling if nothing was happening."

Shriver is an expert, and when all else fails he can rattle off statistics as if his mind were an instant calculating machine. Few attackers can stay with him. As a result, he has managed to make the War on Poverty like the sorcerer's kettle of brew: When the sorcerer's apprentice forgot the magic words, it just went on and on and on . . . brewing. And to keep the kettle brewing it can't be anything but helpful to have two brothers-in-law (Robert and Edward Kennedy) both sitting on the Senate Labor Committee which reviews War on Poverty appropriations!

To Vice President HUBERT HUMPHREY has fallen the ironic job of defending the War on Poverty. Under normal circumstances this would be a congenial task for him, since the Job Corps was originally his "brainchild." But Sargent Shriver, as the brother-in-law of Bobby and Teddy Kennedy, can be expected to line up for one or the other against Humphrey when the chips are down. One astute columnist commented, "The job and pay are improving, but the vice presidential role is becoming decidedly schizophrenic." [29]

Humphrey supports the War on Poverty as he does most things . . . with an eye on Hubert Horatio Humphrey.

The strange, brilliant brain that is SAUL ALINSKY is the most controversial and *indirect* influence in the War on Poverty today. Alinsky-ism can not be ignored . . . it pops up everywhere in this poverty campaign.

Dr. Saul Alinsky doubles as the hard boiled tactician and chief of the guerrilla forces supporting the major revolutionary aspects of the War on Poverty. As a self-styled professional revolutionist, Dr. Alinsky must have felt a deep thrill of satisfaction when President Johnson said:

> "There is going to be a revolution. There is going to be a rising up and throwing off of these [poverty] chains. If a peaceful revolution is not possible, a violent adjustment is inevitable." [30]

Alinsky is bluntly skeptical of the willingness of any government power structure to finance his fiercely militant uprisings of the poor. It is not dif-

ficult to envision Alinsky's half hopeful, half cyni-
cal reaction to President Johnson's explanation of
the financing of the Great Society's blueprint for
revolution:

> "We are going to try to take all the money
> that we think is unnecessarily being spent and
> take it from the 'haves' and give it to the
> 'have nots' that need it so much." [31]

The first sentence from Dr. Alinsky's newest
book, *Rules for Revolution*, reads:

> "Machiavelli wrote *The Prince* to tell the
> 'haves' how to keep it; this is a book to tell
> the 'have nots' how to take it away."

His philosophy is really very simple: "Threats
get you what you want from the government." He
believes that "there can be no social change without
conflict first" [32] and that the federal War on Poverty can not "afford, politically, to finance with
public funds . . . [this] type of agitation, which en-
rages so much of the public and so many local politicians." [33]

Thus Alinsky heads a "guerrilla" War on Poverty outside the formal framework of the federal
program but inside the basic philosophy.

Alinsky's tactics are (1) to organize the minori-
ties into effective political power blocks . . . "People's Organizations," (2) fan complaints into critical "issues," and (3) apply the pressures of rent
strikes, sit-ins, boycotts, and anything else that can
be thought up, in order to get that which is "rightfully" due.

Dr. Alinsky explains that:

> "The fight is in the streets . . . in this revolu-

tion. We know one thing, we know that the only way a people get equality, the only way they get what is rightfully theirs, is when they have the strength or the power to come in and say 'either or else.' " [34]

"Either or else"!

Alinsky learned his tactics in the early days of organizing the CIO. Since then he has been organizing the poor through the work of his controversial training school for agitators, the Industrial Areas Foundation, in Chicago. His whole program is based on the effectiveness of establishing a "power that threatens." Program literature, frequently published with anti-poverty money, is full of such talk as "guerrilla warfare" and "agitation to the point of contact." Applicants for the training program "should have a controlled but intense anger about continued injustice." [35]

For purposes of agitation, his hand has more aces than a pinochle deck. How would you like to play against charges of police brutality, lack of recreational facilities, inadequate garbage disposal, excessive rents, unjustified eviction, demands for civilian police review boards, demands for across-the-board integration of police, fire, and city jobs, de-facto segregation, attacks on any new, tough riot control measures, erasing of police records to render criminals "more employable," minimum wages for migrant farm laborers, and demands that local anti-poverty boards be "controlled" by the poor?

In examining the psychology of minority demands, Los Angeles Superior Court Judge, Richard F. C. Hayden, reasons that "it really doesn't matter if any of their (Negro) complaints are in actuality true . . . the point is that they believe them to be true." [36]

All right, this may seem like a fuzzy line of thinking to you, but the real point is that it has become the foundation upon which many expensive programs are being built.

By constantly pitting the poor against the balance of the community, Alinsky is following close to the old Marxist pattern of class distinction and hate. If a social welfare agency is offering a program, it is bad because it is run by "them." If the federal government is sponsoring a War on Poverty it will fail because it will be run by "them." If "them" includes Negroes, these Negroes are "rubber stamp Toms" chosen by "downtown" people.[37] The only successful formula, according to Alinsky, is to organize the poor so effectively that they can "demand" their due, independent of any government or welfare agency or political party. Independent of the Alinsky influence also?

Dr. Alinsky has been busy at work in Syracuse, where he operated on a federal anti-poverty grant of $314,000 to organize the poor into "effective democratic organizations" (small "d").[38] While block workers were out "organizing," conducting "voter registration drives," and storming "City Hall," their salaries as well as their baby sitting costs were paid for by the taxpayers.[39] Federal funds were used as bail for anti-poverty workers arrested in sit-in demonstrations, all of which (according to Sargent Shriver at the time) was perfectly legal since the Syracuse program had been allocated $5,-000 for "legal" purposes, which naturally included bail.[40] Neat, huh?

Another little project of Alinsky's Syracuse group was a campaign (which you paid for) to get a prisoner released from jail as a victim of poverty. Newspaper accounts described the prisoner as a vicious, habitual criminal whose record included cases of rape, sodomy, and assault.[41]

When these activities began to receive too much

publicity, Sargent Shriver decided a hasty retreat was in line and quietly withdrew anti-poverty funds from Alinsky's Syracuse group.[42] But then this came as no surprise to Dr. Alinsky, nor did it particularly upset him since various councils of churches were more than eager to finance him as a sort of revolutionary patron saint.

Dr. Alinsky has his hand in things in Rochester, New York, where the Rochester Council of Churches hired him for a modest $100,000 to organize the poor of their community.[43] The head of Alinsky's Rochester community organization wore a Malcolm X button and publicly stated, "We intend to see that business will *not* resume as usual for any program affecting blacks in this community."[44]

The ubiquitous Dr. Alinsky is busy in California too, where this past summer he trained 400 ministers under contract to Episcopal and Presbyterian agencies.[45] Alinsky leans heavily on religious establishments to provide him support and respectability in communities, and he apparently has no trouble getting this support. Yet, as the Indianapolis Star commented:

" . . . a long time Leftwinger in politics, Alinsky scorns both political and religious dogma. His talks to the clergy are seasoned with sarcastic comments about organized religion, all of which the ministers appear to gobble up with an almost clinical masochistic glee."[46]

Alinsky was the guest speaker at the tax-supported Los Angeles County Human Relations Commission the month prior to the Watts riots. Along with his usual praises for revolution in the streets, he had high praise for the $18,000 a year executive director of the commission, John Buggs, of whom he said:

"How you go about creating a militant organization when you're being paid by the public authorities, whose main function is to keep down a militant organization, is quite a difficult dilemma . . . [but] I checked with some of my associates and repeatedly got the word back, 'This guy [John Buggs] is okay' . . . and believe me, that is quite a recommendation, coming from the people I was checking with."[47]

Dr. Alinsky is busy organizing the poor in Buffalo and Kansas City, too, and may have some nice contracts in even more cities by the time you read this. His influence is spreading and Sargent Shriver just *can't* ignore it. Activity in Alinsky's Woodlawn Organization in Chicago brought such prominence to Mrs. Gladys Kyles that Shriver appointed her to the 28 member National Advisory Council of the War on Poverty. That's quite an honor for a 38-year-old mother with eleven children who draws approximately $400 a month from Aid-to-Families-with-Dependent-Children and who claims she has not seen her estranged husband since 1957, yet her youngest children are 2, 4, and 5 years old.[48]

Wherever Dr. Alinsky goes he triggers a reflex response of fear and animosity. By intentionally choosing areas of conflict within a community and fanning the sparks of discontent, he can quickly get and hold the attention of minority groups. But in building a community action program on anger and frustration, it is necessary to keep fanning the flames and this demands an outside "enemy."

Dr. Alinsky has created just such a foe. He calls it "City Hall" and it is his favorite target,[49] that is, when he is not too busy denouncing the "haves."

Big time unions and civil rights leaders have been quick to recognize the potential in Alinsky's theories. In Chicago, Walter Reuther's United Auto Workers have committed themselves financially and ideologically to Martin Luther King's Alinsky-type unionization of the poor. The Los Angeles Times on March 10, 1966, reported, "The union agreed to . . . organize slum dwellers into a union which could bargain for better conditions with landlords . . . [and] help civil rights organizations put together a massive voter registration campaign in Negro neighborhoods . . ."

Wonder what they'll call this new union . . . the IOU?

All of this puts PRESIDENT JOHNSON in a most interesting position.

From the beginning, Community Action programs (the "of, by and for the poor" variety) have been the heart of Johnson's War on Poverty, but they have also resulted in the most headaches. These programs have always been viewed as the vehicle for "social revolution" to be used by militant leaders to transform life in the Negro ghettos. They are important to the civil rights movement which Johnson is so committed to support. But his big city Democrat machines, which he obviously must support, aren't very happy about having their power challenged by a federally financed organization of the poor.

As Commander-in-Chief of the entire Great Society he can not afford to let single battles splinter the overall battle plan. Judging from his 1966 State of the Union speech, the President now envisions his Great Society as world-wide. His generous "Head Start" plan in his new international War on Poverty has only one flaw. It appears that the only "haves" he plans to take from are the Americans, while the "have nots" he intends to give to are "international" . . . the whole of the "have not" world. Nuts!

Chapter Three

PANDORA'S CAP

COMMUNITY ACTION PROGRAMS (CAP) have done more to confuse the already muddy picture of administrating the War on Poverty than almost any other section of the law. Examples of what *is* happening in CAP programs are so shocking that there's hardly any shock left over for what *can* happen.

Community Action projects can be thought up by a group of *unelected* people using federal tax money to finance their latest brainchild.[1] Senator Peter Dominick says simply, "The problem is . . . that a group of idealistic citizens can form a corporation and suddenly start working on a particular project with federal funds, which may be wholly unrealistic . . . if there ever was a specific issue which needs to be controlled, this is it; namely a community action program sponsored and developed by a local non-governmental unit.[2]

Briefly, for any program to qualify under this section of the law, it must do three things:

(1) Be large enough in scope to hold promise of helping to alleviate poverty,

(2) Be "developed, conducted, and administered with the maximum, feasible participation" of the poor, and,

(3) Be conducted by a public or private non-profit agency.[3]

Guidelines from Sargent Shriver's office have indicated that each community should have an anti-poverty "broad based" agency to screen and coordinate various local proposals. However, "community," has never been satisfactorily defined, nor has "broad based" been spelled out, so right off the bat you have controversy.

How big is a "community?" Is it a city? A group of cities? A county? A group of counties? Perhaps even a state?

Who establishes these anti-poverty agencies? What if more than one vies for Washington's recognition?

Does "maximum participation" of the poor mean that the poor should have voting control over which programs are approved and which are not? Or does it merely mean that the poor should have fair representation on the local anti-poverty board? If so, who decides what "fair" is? How are the poor to be chosen for their participation on the board? By appointment or by election?

Does the local anti-poverty board have jurisdiction over all titles of the Economic Opportunity

Act, or are they to administer only Title I-A (Community Action)?

If a non-profit organization, a church group for example, wishes to seek federal financing for a poverty program, do they first have to have approval from the local anti-poverty agency? Or can they, as they are doing now, apply directly to Washington?

Questions like these could go on and on and on. The law simply doesn't answer any of them. Guidelines from boss Shriver's bureaucracy have been as flexible as they have been numerous. Double talk and tight rope walking are plentiful; specific answers no one can get. The result is that arguments and bitter controversy have pitted one group against another in a frenzied desire to get its hands on the fatted pig.

Community coordinating councils of one type or another usually have led the way in setting up these unelected poverty agencies to run the war, but despite this built-in machinery for promotional structure, the result has been havoc. Civil rights workers battle with social workers. Local government contends with federal government. One church group vies with another. One community resents its neighbor. The Mexican-Americans feel that the Negroes are receiving more than their share, while the Negroes claim that the Mexican-Americans don't need as much. The "poor" are pitted against the "power structure."

One group, however, is always left out of the slightest consideration. It is the average taxpayer who has nothing to gain but a larger tax bill, less representation, and an awful headache from trying to understand the whole mess.

Supposedly the cost of these programs is to be shared on a 90-10% basis . . . that is, the federal government will pay 90% and the community or participating agency is to meet this amount with the remaining 10% of the program cost.⁴ Eventually, so it is said, the split will drop to a 50-50 share-the-cost basis. Originally this was to happen in the fall of 1966, but last year that deadline was extended to August, 1967. By that date, Community Action programs should be firmly established, and taxpayers' yowls at having to cough up 50% of the financing for these extravagant programs will likely be considered as just so many sour grapes in a luscious bunch.

However we are convinced that this 50-50 sharing requirement will *never* come about. Communities tend to take a closer look at the cost of these programs when they think their local taxes might have to support 50% of the cost (apparently it is assumed by many that federal tax money doesn't cost the taxpayers anything), and a close look is hardly what a patronage-filled program desires. Then too, the real control rests with whoever controls the purse strings, and federal bureaucracy has no intention of selling itself short.

To quickly summarize before we go into what *kind* of programs you are financing through Community Action, we will simply say that BILLIONS of federal tax dollars are going to *non-elected* groups, who are responsible to no one but themselves and Sargent Shriver, to set up and run just about any kind of program you can think of.

When the citizen discovers that his tax dollars are financing a blueprint for revolution sponsored by pressure groups of a certain political leaning, there is no recourse through locally elected officials because they are not required to be responsible. When he discovers that socialism and communism are being taught and paid for with his tax dollars,* he has no recourse through his local school board, because school boards are not required to administer these programs. He may discover that his money is being used to sponsor rent strikes or school boycotts. But he will also discover that he has no place to go to voice his objections.

The concerned citizen can, of course, complain to Washington, but the age of "Mr. Smith Goes to Washington" seems lost forever in a maze of expensive corridors, lavishly furnished but closed-door hearing rooms, and the misconception that Congress rather than the White House still legislates in the Capitol.

We have deliberately not said "if" these things are discovered. Let's look at some of the facts in this War on Poverty and see why.

Three years ago the late President Kennedy launched the pilot project for the War on Poverty.[5] Mobilization for Youth (MFY) was the private non-profit organization set up to carry out a program designed to cut delinquency, poverty, and crime in a 20 block area of New York's lower East Side. Over a three year period of time it was to receive $8 million in federal funds, plus $2.8 million from the city, and $2 million from the Ford Foundation.[6] Built on the latest social theories to be had from the universities, the late President described it as "the most advanced program yet devised to combat delinquency on a broad scale."[8] (In all fairness to this program it was never billed as a program to combat political delinquency.)

The New York Times enthusiastically described this venture as "part of a program designed to strike eventually at the roots of the national juvenile delinquency problem."[9] In July of 1964, President Johnson announced another $1.5 million federal grant to MFY for training drop-outs and declared it had his "deep interest and support,"[10] as did his larger program along the same lines, the War on Poverty, due to pass Congress one month later.

In the fall of 1964, two years and $10 million tax dollars after the launching of this first anti-poverty missile, the New York Daily News made an investigation. Charges were made (and later substantiated by the FBI) that: More than 37 MFY employees had subversive or communist backgrounds;[11] James E. McCarthy (MFY Administrator who shortly resigned for "health" reasons) had spent $23,000 of agency funds for dinners, hotels, and other creature comforts;[12] agency facilities had been used to foment school boycotts, rent strikes, and racial disorders.[13]

So what had this pilot program of the War on Poverty really accomplished in over two years and with more than $12 million? It had sponsored or made available facilities for radical political action such as rent strikes led by communists. (An identified communist agent, Jesse Gray, served the agency as a "rent strike expert consultant.")[14] It had recruited for Bayard Rustin (pacifist, former Young Communist, convicted sex pervert, and organizer of New York's infamous March on Washington in 1963.[15] It had given its enthusiastic support to 500 members for his first school boycott)[16] All of these activities, which you were paying for, were, we are to assume, supposed to prepare slum dwellers for "participation in community life."

MFY's executives had lavish expense accounts, and its subversives had refuge as well as financing.

The whole basis of MFY's approach was to challenge the existing American concepts by defying law and order in the style and manner of Marxist revolutionaries.

MFY's officials boasted and bragged of the distinction they were achieving as President Johnson's War on Poverty pioneers . . . and who can argue with them? They said that they were personally staffing a similar Harlem organization which proposed to spend $119 million of anti-poverty funds, and that they were sending personnel to other organizations outside of the state.[17] And who can doubt them, since their mark of style can now be spotted across the nation?

Sociologists continue to cite MFY's "outstanding contributions" in demonstrating "new and effective methods."[18] In July of 1965 (months after the conclusive FBI investigation) the Senate Labor and Public Welfare Committee quietly approved the funding of $6.5 million of your money to MFY and other "community action projects."[19] On January 9, 1966, a UPI news release told of a new consumer education program conducted by MFY which is attempting to educate the poor in the ways of "unscrupulous merchants and loan sharks."[20]

MFY—Mobilization for Youth—is still well fed and going strong.

Now that the first anti-poverty missile had been successfully launched and was in orbit, the gold rush into space was on.

For example, when a federal anti-poverty grant of $230,000 was given to a New York agency, the officials (already salaried at $12,000 to $20,000 a year) promptly took off for a weekend at an expensive resort in the Adirondacks to "study the juvenile delinquency problem in the New York area."[21] Sound MFY familiar?

While these officials were up there their expense account totaled over $2,000 for refreshments ("booze" in the Congressional Record) and rooms at the plush resort. Also present were six "consultants" drawing $75 a day plus all expenses for the two days they were there. Even rental of tuxedos and flowers was charged to their expense account. Telephone bills ranged from $113 to $331.[22] Senator John L. Williams said:

> "I do not know whom they were telephoning, unless they were calling Washington to explain what a terrific job they were doing; or is it possible that they were calling to discuss what a wonderful time they were having?"[23]

Obviously, the lesson of MFY's successful $23,000 budget for dinners and hotel stops was well learned. But what about MFY's examples of "community action" in demonstrations, racial rioting, and party politics? These lessons, too, were quickly picked up from this pilot project.

Tax supplied poverty funds financed a march of 200 demonstrators from Philadelphia to the capitol of Pennsylvania during the summer of 1965.[24] In addition to such expensive excursions, your tax money paid the $17,000 a year salary of Charles Bowser, the aggressive head of the Philadelphia Anti-Poverty Committee. Bowser led the demonstrators who stationed themselves at the door of the governor's office chanting "Show your face, show your face."[25]

In the War on Poverty, "community action" appears to by-pass *asking* for an interview with your governor. You just stand at his door and yell, "Show your face." It may be constitutional, but it is certainly something new as a way of solving grievances in America.

The Office of Economic Opportunity said it did not know the Philadelphia agency had used poverty funds to charter busses and pay other expenses for the demonstrations. But it was done and it is being done throughout our nation, and nothing, really, seems to be done about it.

In Syracuse, Mayor William Walsh, an early supporter of the poverty program, has learned what San Francisco's Mayor John Shelley meant when he accused the Office of Economic Opportunity of "trying to wreck local government by setting the poor against City Hall."[26]*

A federal anti-poverty grant of $314,000 was given to Syracuse University (bypassing the city anti-poverty agency) to develop "effective democratic organizations in low-income areas."[27] As you recall, in Chapter Two we met Dr. Saul Alinsky, who was appointed director of this University program. In that chapter we discussed the type of political programs in which this Syracuse pressure group was involved . . . the use of tax money to bail demonstrators and criminals out of jail, to pay baby sitters while the poor were out storming City Hall, and to do almost anything to promote social revolution.

Mayor Walsh charged that there were voter registration drives paid for with poverty money to get the poor to register as Democrats.[28] It seems printed instructions to the block workers (working on tax financed salaries) told them that when they rang the doorbell they were to say, "We are here to strengthen democratic institutions and or-

*Columnist Casper Weinberger reports that Mayor John Shelley yielded last fall to demands, reinforced by threats of demonstrations and picketing, that representatives of the poor have the controlling voice in San Francisco's War on Poverty, not only in the designated neighborhoods, but also on the city-wide Economic Council and its executive board.[29]

ganizations." "Democratic" was spelled with a small "d."

Now just exactly *how* can a voice capitalize or uncapitalize a letter? Orally it comes out, "We are here to strengthen Democratic organizations."

Here's to the War on Poverty . . . and also, as a mere side issue, a bigger and stronger Democrat Party machine.

There is one anti-poverty agency that has perhaps received more money, more publicity, and more defense than any other organization in this War on Poverty. Harlem's HARYOU-ACT, which is reported to have received over $100 million for its poverty programs, is the militant civil rights organization referred to as "just one more of Adam Clayton Powell's expensive little hobbies."[30] Expensive yes, but definitely not little.

HARYOU-ACT has given birth to a group known as the "Five Percenters." This group gets its name from the belief that only 5% of the Negro race truly understands, and is truly dedicated to, the revolutionary struggle.[31] Eighty-five percent of the Negroes, they cry, are dogs, exploited and glad to be exploited. Ten percent are exploiters themselves. That leaves the Five Percenters, expertly trained in judo and karate, who apparently have managed to terrorize large parts of Harlem and have been successfully blackmailing city and federal governments. "Continue to pour money into us through HARYOU-ACT," they say in effect, "or else we will bring bloody revolution to the streets of New York."*

Even the militant civil rights director of HARYOU-ACT, Livingston Wingate (close friend

*In Harlem the Boy Scouts are considered "square and middle class," according to Kenneth Marshall, HARYOU-ACT program director.[34]

and one time aide of Adam Clayton Powell) seems frightened by the genii emerging from his political jar:

"I've talked to the police. They're scared, they know the facts. If I tell too much I'll be the late Wingate."[32]

William F. Buckley, Jr., editor of *National Review*, suggests that:

"The scandal in the making is the rumor that important politicians, state, city and federal, have known about the blackmail but, for fear of igniting a riot, have gone along with it."[33]

Crime does not pay? Or is it more reasonable to believe that certain types of crime are being permitted to pay?

HARYOU-ACT has consistently urged the establishment of a civilian police review board,[35] and newly elected Mayor John Lindsay has eagerly bowed to the demand. By way of explanation, the Mayor said that the civilian review board issue is "highly symbolic to minority groups", and that providing one will help "take the edge off the tension" in Harlem.[36] Lindsay thus paved the way for his new police commissioner, Howard R. Leary, a Philadelphian who is well versed in the working of civilian review boards. While Leary feels such a board has been completely successful in Philadelphia, the police department there doesn't quite agree . . . seems they are having a heck of a time recruiting policemen![37] If New York street crime takes an upswing, the blame could well be put on Lindsay's review board by showing it has made policemen reluctant to make arrests for fear of being accused of brutality . . . or even reluctant to become policemen in the first place.

HARYOU-ACT has attacked the public schools as having permitted themselves to "become contaminated by the moral sickness of racism."[38] (Keep that remark in mind when you read later about another little project of HARYOU-ACT, the Black Arts Repertory Theater . . . the shoe is on the other foot there, and the fit is completely different.) Dr. Kenneth B. Clark, widely known Negro psychologist, writes in the 614 page HARYOU-ACT report that was the result of an 18 month research program financed with tax money:

"The public schools have permitted their procedures, programs, and practices to reflect the fact that in our society, people who are perceived as lacking power are pushed around, ignored, excluded or relegated to secondary priority status . . .

"American public schools have developed different standards of education and expectation for lower status groups and thereby have been accessories to the reinforcement of a system of cruelty, injustice, and arbitrary rejection which spawns human casualties and social pathology."[39]

There's some interesting food for thought in that attack.

In the process of all of this social psychoanalysis, HARYOU-ACT managed to overdraw its bank account by $207,000 and run up another $200,000 in unpaid bills. Sargent Shriver rushed a $400,000 retroactive appropriation to Harlem to save the program from collapse and sent in federal auditors to examine the ledger.[40] But District Attorney Frank Hogan stepped in ahead and subpoenaed the books. By October, 1965, he had already found serious irregularities . . . namely that the directors could not account for about $800,000 of your tax money.[41] When the internationally known audit company of Price-Waterhouse was called in, they said they could not proceed because they could not find sufficient books with which to conduct an audit!

The list of scandalous activities of HARYOU-ACT parallels MFY, but the most recent escapade is worth mentioning . . . just to curl your hair.

The "Black Arts Repertory Theater" received $40,000 through HARYOU-ACT for its eight week program of training and shows. According to a December 1, 1965, Associated Press news release:

"Each night in a makeshift Harlem theater a group of young Negroes give vent to their hatred of 'Whitey' . . . Chalked-faced Negroes perform the roles of whites, frequently portrayed as homosexuals, in these Black Arts Theater dramas . . ."

This tax supported anti-poverty school is coached by the violence-preaching Negro playwright, LeRoi Jones, who says "I don't see anything wrong with hating white people."[42] He has led demonstrations denouncing city and federal investigations of HARYOU-ACT and in one such protest he assailed the white man as "a loathsome beast."[43] To his questionable reputation as a playwright he has plays like "The Toilet" and "The Dutchman" about which the *New Yorker* says the "wit is curdled by spite."[44]

Two dozen writers, sculptors and painters teach at this school and 12 to 15 actors form the core of the repertory company. Apparently, it is upon hatred of the white, and not upon any positive values, that they base their pride in the Negro race. Lines from one production read:

"The white man cannot deny when we met him he was living in a cave, walking around on his hands and knees, and eating raw meat. He couldn't hardly use his vocal cords. It was the white man who was civilized by the black man. We are the most intelligent, wisest people on this planet."[45]

As an excuse for this use of tax money to finance a psychotic program, we will quote, without comment (and that takes self-control), James Kelleher, Deputy Director of Publicity for the Office of Economic Opportunity:

"We'd rather see these kids fussing on the stage than on the streets . . . this was a part of *Project Uplift* we funded through HAR-YOU-ACT last summer . . . the overall program was a good one and we have to figure that this [the theater school] was a part of its success . . .

"HARYOU-ACT wanted Jones in the program. He is a legitimate playwright, whatever you may think about his views. We knew about it when we granted the money and *we have no apologies.*"[46] (our emphasis)

Chapter Four

THE BYPASS PLAY

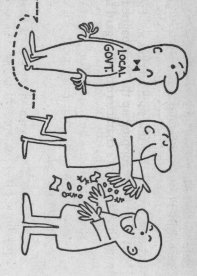

Now we come to a red hot issue in this "war": The manner in which the federal government is passing out "free" money directly to the people without touching base with locally elected officials. What's behind it all?

Suddenly the authority to solve community problems with tax money has become a matter strictly up to a group of unelected citizens and a federal bureaucracy. Freed from having to face the electorate, economy is seldom an issue and these self-appointed citizens and their bureaucratic allies make a great partnership employing a whole new set of rules and values.

What is happening to our fundamental respect for local government? What happens when all the restraints upon the federal government are dropped in history's ashcan?

First of all, the most dull witted public official ought to be able to see that he is writing his own political death warrant by allowing the federal government to reduce him and his colleagues to the role of an administrative puppet. The tragic fact, however, is that few such officials are fighting. Most of them are sopping up the champagne money with the drunkard's characteristic disregard for the morning-after.

Congressman Don Clausen, while fighting on the House floor to amend the law to preserve at least some local control, said:

"Above all . . . representatives of local government should have the maximum opportunity to have a say in any governmental program—if anyone is entitled to a veto power, it should be these elected officials, be they mayor, supervisor, or councilmen . . . One of the great dangers of this bill lies in the possible circumvention of local and state authorities."[1]

Secondly, the public itself seems perfectly willing to allow its locally elected officials to commit suicide. Actually, murder and suicide would express it better because when our local officials are snuffed out, our freedom goes with them.

The something-for-nothing idea is terribly appealing, even when you're adult enough to know there's usually a catch. In this case, it can be a fatal catch, that is unless you believe in a central government dictatorship.

For a community to solve its own problems within its own fiscal limitation is becoming a thing of the past. Well financed federal bureaucrats are ready and eager to take over, convinced that they know what is best for all. As long as their local partner is completely dependent upon them for financing, guess which will be the "senior" partner!

Plaintive cries from a few mayors and councilmen and supervisors that tax money is financing their destruction apparently aren't disturbing Washington too much. For everyone who complains, there are three or four who are in on the Great Society's sleigh ride, and as someone once said, "You have to break some eggs to make an omelet." Sargeant Shriver puts it more bluntly: "We are in the midst of a revolution."[2] "Hallelujah, a revolution!

If you are old enough to believe that a vital republic must be based on strong, elected, local institutions, then you're just not with the Great Society. We taxpayers get only one break: Our times have produced a tender technique. We won't be hanged, just hypnotized.

Local volunteer programs are bound to find themselves threatened by abandonment when all of this poorly directed federal money pours in. Who will continue to support the Salvation Army, Youth Clubs, the YMCA, once it is discovered that the federal government is out-promising, if not out-performing them, right down the line—*without* asking for local money or volunteers?

Congressman H. Allen Smith points out where an even greater (and more immediate) trouble lies:

"Local welfare agencies, both public and private . . . are concerned over losses of their trained social workers to newly established groups supported by federal funds. The federal programs come along, offer more money, and the local agencies lose their qualified personnel."[3]

Many of these fine volunteer organizations have tried sipping of the tempting federal funds themselves. Some have already felt the first pinches of the inevitable federal control which federal officials renounce until established. Others have felt the reaction of the taxpayer who feels he cannot *give* from his charity pocket to organizations which are already *taking* from his tax pocket.

Left on their own, Americans have traditionally been generous and soft-hearted, almost to the point of naivete. We have preferred naivete to selfishness. But now the government has declared human welfare to be solely *its* responsibility. Welfare has become all mixed up in red tape and regulations and "rights," and compassion has been replaced by bitterness. Ironically, the bitterness is shared by those who receive, who say "It's owed me," as well as by those who provide, who wail "I'm being taxed out of my home."

We are on the verge of completely losing our fine historic sense of personal charity and responsibility, by accepting the premise that the government is the sole guardian of the unfortunate members of society. The Great Society doesn't need the benevolent hand of the charitable giver. It has tax collectors backed up by armed force and it will do our giving for us.

So tempting is this "free" money (our money, or what's left of it by the time it gets back from Washington), that many of the locally *elected* agencies have quietly rationalized their drinking from the intoxicating fountain. If we don't use it, they say, someone else will, and after all it is our money and we might as well get back as much as we can. This reaction being typically cosmopolitan, the Great Society knew exactly what it was doing when it held out the bait. Think of those few isolated dreamers who thought this money would go where it was needed the most!

How familiar the oft-repeated refrain, as expressed by Robert E. Jenkins, Superintendent of Schools in Pasadena: "Congress has enacted the law and appropriated the funds. The President has signed the bill. It behooves our city to be in the lead to use the funds. After all, the money's there and if we don't use it some other city will."[4] And this from the superintendent of one of the most expensive school systems in the State of California![5]

So with the cushiony encouragement of such words, school boards, eager to improve their remedial programs and fascinated by the promises of all the things they think they can't afford, have convinced themselves that there is no danger of federal control. If so, they argue, they will simply refuse any more federal money, so there!

It is pure folly to think a school board can simply refuse to continue federally financed poverty programs once they have started. Just envision the civil rights yowls that would ensue if a program were dropped . . . pickets, demonstrations and school boycotts that would, in all probability, be financed by anti-poverty money!

But accepting federal aid has been rationalized and rationalized and rationalized . . . as no doubt Adam did when he betook himself of Eve's apple.

When the Pasadena School Board went along with their Superintendent in taking $681,000 for a federally financed poverty program, only one board member hesitated. Steve Salisian predicted that "the day will come when the federal government will attach a condition."[6]

Communities opposed to the expense and principle of cross-town bussing for the sole purpose of alleviating de-facto segregation are beginning to realize that their preference for neighborhood schools will have to go if federal money is to continue to come.

The State of Illinois accepted $61.7 million in federal funds for projects to provide special educational services to educationally deprived children of low-income families. Enter: A Chicago group, called the Co-ordinating Council of Community Organizations, which has long advocated cross-town bussing and has been the promoter of mass street demonstrations protesting alleged de-facto segregation. Late in September, 1965, the group filed a complaint in Washington charging the Chicago schools with non-compliance to the 1964 Civil Rights Act. Francis Keppel, United States Education Commissioner, immediately ordered the withholding of Chicago's $30 million share of the federal funds until the *alleged* discrimination was halted.[7]

The Superintendent of Chicago's public schools, Benjamin C. Willis, said, "It is an alarming and threatening kind of procedure ... At no time, even now, have I received any indication of what the complaints are or what the probable noncompliances are."[8]

The Illinois State Superintendent of Public Instruction, Ray Page, said that he had not been advised about any complaints concerning Chicago's school system. He added, "No investigator [from the U.S. Office of Education] has called upon me and I am completely uninformed as to the specific charges. What noncompliance is alleged?"[9]

Democrat Mayor Richard J. Daley reacted violently, charging that the action had done "irreparable damage to the whole concept of federal aid to education."[10] He called Keppel's action "indiscreet" and reportedly took his anger straight to the White House. The White House, visibly upset at the premature and "indiscreet" snapping of the mouse trap, ordered immediate release of the funds.[11]

It is interesting to note that early in 1965 the NAACP in Boston, Mass., said that it intended to challenge the local use of anti-poverty funds because a large portion was to be handled by the school system, which they asserted is illegally operating racially imbalanced schools, "If we get the answer we seek," the NAACP said in a statement, "the whole anti-poverty campaign will grind to a halt in many cities until the school segregation problem is solved."[12]

In November, 1965, President Johnson ordered the Civil Rights Commission to start immediately on a study of de-facto segregation in public schools.[13] This study, and the recommendations for federal action that will come with it, will put the administration squarely in the middle of one of the most sensitive social issues in the nation: Should white and Negro children be denied, because of the color of their skin, the right to attend the school closest to them? Should they be transported out of their neighborhoods, not to alleviate overcrowded schools, but merely to achieve racially balanced schools?

If the federal government decides in favor of crosstown bussing to correct de-facto segregation, there will be a heavy club held over those school boards which disagree, even if it means some kind of inter-district arrangement. The club? Withdrawal of federal money. And it will be like David facing Goliath with an empty slingshot.

Adam Clayton Powell spelled it out in an official press release on December 9, 1965:

"Directly related to the War on Poverty is the battle against de-facto segregation in public schools.

"Black people are not going to passively accept much longer the hypocrisy of federal spending to decrease poverty along with federal spending to increase de-facto segregation . . .

"The Committee on Education and Labor will definitely conduct hearings on de-facto segregation when Congress reconvenes with the intention of writing new legislation to deal with it. This will be one of the major bills of this Committee next year."

And what Adam wants, Adam usually gets.

How can school boards, such as Pasadena's, elected by an overwhelming majority on a platform opposed to cross-town bussing for ethnic balance, continue to rush headlong into federal programs?

"There are always strings attached to shiny packages of federal goodies . . . Our grandfathers . . . would have recognized arbitrary federal interference with the right of local individuals to govern themselves . . . as a long step toward tyranny . . . Nobody ever said that local control of our own affairs was more economical than statism, or more efficient, or more honest . . . It's just FREER . . . It's always been expensive . . . expensive in terms of money and sometimes in terms of human lives. But to the men who fought the King, the Redcoats, Hessians, the Indians . . . 200 years ago to gain freedom for their children, local self-government was worth whatever it cost . . . So sit back . . . It's so much more convenient to let Washington handle these details . . . This is the way empires are lost, and independence, and individual liberty."

Dr. Max Rafferty
Calif. State Supt. of Public Instruction
November 28, 1965

There are, or were, a few staunchly independent

communities left which never considered themselves poverty-stricken and therefore never considered having to accept federal anti-poverty money. A small township in Michigan was just such a community. Ypsilanti's story flamed across the nation early in the summer of 1965. But after months of frustrating defeat, the fires of resistance eventually went out and resignation set in. Ypsilanti's story is in the past tense, but it is worth repeating for the benefit of other Ypsilantis to come. Senator Peter Dominick said, "It is an account of the most outrageous type of scheme proposed in the name of poverty that I have ever heard."*

In January, 1965, Ypsilanti was declared a poverty area by a group calling themselves WRAND and supposedly representing the Township of Ypsilanti. But apparently WRAND was not an organization of 400 residents of Ypsilanti as it claimed, but of six people, four of whom were connected with the University of Michigan (which was contracting with the federal government to run the $188,000 poverty show in Ypsilanti).

In the initial report sent to Washington, professorial WRAND stated that "Ypsilanti is an impoverished community without social services . . . There is no medical facility, no newspaper, no self-government, no recreational or cultural or even entertainment facility. . . . There are no stores in the area, and schools are a bus ride away."

Startled when it discovered it had practically been declared a disaster area, the good folk of Ypsilanti Township were certain it was a simple matter of mistaken identity . . . someone had just made one of those believe-it-or-not mistakes. They

*Senator Dominick's quote and the following account of the Ypsilanti story is from the Congressional Record, August 18, 1965 (pgs. 20085-20089).

looked at their new modern shopping center, their schools, parks, and movie theater, just to make sure they hadn't disappeared. And yes, they still had a Board of Supervisors. They even had an average income, which, at close to $9,000, was far above the national average.

Even more unbelievable for a town with not one unpaved street were phrases like "the present ghost town appearance" and "brush has overgrown the streets and roads."

The WRAND report went on to advocate "establishing a community vegetable field to be run by the residents on a cooperative basis, with the produce available to the residents for their own consumption"!

Despite repeated efforts on the part of Ypsilanti Township to convince the University of Michigan and the federal government that some horrible mistake had been made, the grant was awarded, the programs even praised by Sargent Shriver, and Ypsilanti is now an example of an "urban fringe pocket of poverty" being revitalized.

Anger was rampant in Ypsilanti: We tell our children to tell the truth . . . if funds have been received on the basis of false statements, those funds should be returned.

The University of Michigan's author of the program replied, "Suppose instead of 'no' stores, we say 'few' stores? Suppose instead of 'no' facilities, we say 'inadequate' facilities?"

Washington sent an official to investigate (*after* the funds had been granted, of course), who said, "Now I want to know what kind of proposal, satisfactory to you, I can take to the University." He went on to explain that since contracts for professional directors had already been let and other commitments had been made, there really wasn't much the Office of Economic Opportunity could do except see that certain errors in the report were corrected, refined, and brought up to date.

"Would that satisfy you?" he asked.

Ypsilanti Supervisor Roy Smith replied, "All that would satisfy me is the return of any poverty money intended for Ypsilanti Township and a public apology to the people here."

To which he was told, "I'm sure the University won't go for anything like that."

And it didn't.

Oh well, people in their towns and counties and states may continue to make a few decisions, but decisions that count will be made by some other men in some other place where the purse strings are held.

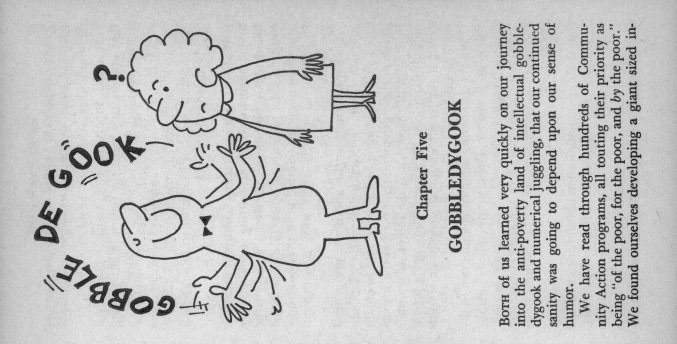

Chapter Five

GOBBLEDYGOOK

BOTH of us learned very quickly on our journey into the anti-poverty land of intellectual gobble-dygook and numerical juggling, that our continued sanity was going to depend upon our sense of humor.

We have read through hundreds of Community Action programs, all touting their priority as being "of the poor, for the poor, and *by* the poor." We found ourselves developing a giant sized inferiority complex as we read through these poverty proposals and kept coming across such paragraphs as:

"Thus, the elemental presupposition implicit in the very existence of the agency ab initio is a set of behavior and condition norms and criteria which assign to the client some level or degree of abjection, the abduration of which is deemed essential to society's well being and progress."[1]

We have to assume that any "culturally deprived, lower economic indigent" sitting on a poverty board about to approve taxpayers' money to be spent on some program or other ($185,000 in the case of the program referred to in the above quotation) knows exactly what such a paragraph means. But we don't.

Such paragraphs as the above are the general rule rather than the exception. Even the most dedicated citizen, assuming he has been able to obtain copies of these programs, soon reaches the frustration point. Perhaps that is the intent. It is rather difficult to criticize (or approve) a program intelligently if you have been put to sleep by an eruditical mish mash.

We are considering submitting a program to the Office of Economic Opportunity called SOUSE: Society for the Ordinary Use of Simple English. To put it "very simply," in the kind of language they seem to understand, we will explain to them that:

"The communication of information, albeit orally or in writing, is immeasurably encumbered through utilization of excessive, superfluous polysyllabics and extraneous intricacies of syntax, resulting in garbled semantic comprehension by, and incomplete dialogue with, the recipients of such information, and, in essence, reflects a predilection on the part of the communicant to demonstrate his superlative erudition, unless, of course, necessitated by the exigencies of the communicative environment or the hyper-complexities of the data being communicated."

How about that? Such a program, so simple in its expressed goal, would probably be a lead pipe cinch to be funded!

Honestly though, Community Action programs include just about anything a group can dream up that can be worded to qualify as "fighting the ills of poverty." The vagueness of language seems to be the protection against duplication charges. A recent grant of over $1 million to the general area of Watts in Los Angeles included such programs as:[2]

"$11,495 to survey potentials for improvement."

"$129,960 to initiate community centers."

"$19,983 to strengthen neighborhood centers and increase neighborhood services."

"$146,805 to provide a technical assistance staff to develop War on Poverty proposals." (!)

"$81,368 for a neighborhood leadership program."

"$67,022 to establish decentralized multi-functional information." (?)

Using the "old" math methods, this adds up to over half a million to sort of look into things, kind of, in a whatcha-ma-call-it way.

A previous list of over 75 programs funded prior to this grant and costing over $10 million included variations of the same theme with the addition of two or three "complaint outposts" in Watts.[3] Costing you $128,000, these Watts "complaint outposts" (in operation the six months prior to the horrible Watts riots) certainly gave no warnings of the complaints that were so pervertedly expressed in the August holocaust.

It is next to impossible to figure out how much has been given to whom to do what. There are training programs, employment guidance programs, consumer education programs, family counseling, centers and outposts, and so on and so forth.

Even the sources of funding are a nightmare of entanglements. Anti-poverty programs can, and do, apply for money not only from the Economic Opportunity Act, but also from the Manpower Development and Training Act, the Juvenile Delinquency and Youth Offenses Control Act, the Vocational Education Act, the Elementary and Secondary Education Act, etc. etc. and etc. Combinations can also be worked . . . that is, some money from one and some from another. And since the left hand in Bureaucracyland seldom knows what the right hand is doing; it can all be for the same program and the chances of anyone ever knowing about it are slim.

The Office of Economic Opportunity was so confused by all of these funding sources that they spent some $70,000 to investigate the laws now on the books dealing with anti-poverty programs.[4] The resulting mammoth report—larger than any Sears catalog—must have proven somewhat embarrassing to the generals of poverty. Instead of 4 or 5 various laws, 94 different laws and programs were uncovered . . . all dealing with anti-poverty and many of which the bureaucrats had forgotten were on the books!

The Wall Street Journal, however, topped this

by discovering 115 federal aid laws and "if subcategories are included the total swells to *216.*"[5]

There's even an encyclopedia of U.S. Government benefits which tells how the individual may bring his future requirements to the government's attention. Columnist Russel Kirk cried out, "Harken to these secular tidings of great joy—you too can live at Government expense!"[6]

We are convinced that in Los Angeles alone it would be virtually impossible to chart all of the anti-poverty programs in any intelligent fashion, especially after the Watts riots when there was such a rush for federal money that the stampede was strictly the every-man-for-himself variety.

Nevertheless, we tried to make such a chart. Our efforts included the expenditure of $1.25 for a large poster board, four days of concentrated research amid our four notebooks of newspaper clippings and a three-drawer filing cabinet stuffed to overflowing from over a year of attending meetings, writing letters, and dogged research, and finally, one bottle of aspirin. We sadly labeled our pathetic result "The Idiot Maze" and finished the bottle of aspirin.

Stripped of their "poverty language," the general run of Community Action programs provides as much pathetic humor as does the CAP program aimed at motivating school drop-outs to return to school, called JOIN, which had to create a sub-program called RE-JOIN to motivate the drop-outs who had dropped out of the drop-out program not to drop out.

The Los Angeles Travelers Aid Society is operating a 24-hour mobile unit to assist poverty-stricken migrants who get lost on our freeways. Honest! And such an invaluable service is all thanks to $202,976 of your War on Poverty money.[7]

A $227,000 proposal for a Vocational Rehabilitation Center[8] to "rehabilitate the mentally and physically disabled" turned out to involve *no* teaching of any kind of vocational skills and wasn't even similar to the fine workshops so needed for our truly physically handicapped people. It was a "pre-vocational" program to train untrained people to be trainable. After two or three months of "counseling and guidance," we were told, these people would be motivated "to keep an appointment on time", and to "learn to fill out application cards" (at the unemployment department?). After achieving these skills they could then be sent to a training center where supposedly they would be trained in some more advanced arts, such as cleaning spark plugs or slapping on whitewash, perhaps.

Included in the budget of this center, where *no* vocational skills were to be taught, was $11,000 for "equipment." Instruction sheets on how to set an alarm clock, maybe?

When we noted that the definition of "mentally handicapped" seemed to be intermingled with "*vocationally* handicapped," we asked what we thought was a bitterly sarcastic question: "Would a person who is just plain lazy be eligible for this program?"

The answer we received was, "Why, of course! Laziness is a serious mental condition which definitely constitutes a vocational handicap."

Try arguing with that!

How about an adult education program for 120 persons that costs more than it would to send private tutors to the homes of each of the 120? And *twenty* times as much as an existing, locally financed, program![9]

The once famous Pasadena Community Playhouse has requested three quarters of a million dollars to provide, among other things, tent shows for the culturally deprived. The request reads:

"The concept of the Great Society does not limit itself to the relief of the economic ills alone. It embraces the economic, social and cultural growth and well-being of all who are presently disadvantaged. The theater, therefore, which through the ages has nourished the spirit of man, must be available to all . . . If culture is good for some it is good for all."[10]

Possibly we should consider that if paying for theater tickets with tax money is good for some it is good for all.

Speaking of culture, Senator Everett Dirksen ripped into the poverty program by saying, "We have agriculture . . . horticulture . . . silviculture . . . social culture . . . now we have the culture of poverty."[11]

What had so appalled the senator was the hiring of some 2,000 college graduates to study the "Culture of Poverty."

"Is that not wonderful?" Dirksen asked his colleagues. "Some 2,152 fine young college graduates looking like an arrow collar ad, coming down here to get the culture of poverty. And they will go abroad in the land, in the hinterland, and in the metropolitan center. They will talk with people and they say, 'Don't you know about the culture of poverty?' The people will say, 'All we know is that we owe the grocer . . . the meat market . . . an installment on a second hand automobile . . . so what is this business about the Culture of Poverty?' The Culture of Poverty is a fine sounding phrase, but it will not fool the American people."[12]

We hope not. But then, we can't be sure. We never took the complete course.

All of this may sound as ridiculous to you as it did to Senator Dirksen, but the painful truth is that studying the Culture of Poverty is THE thing today. It is being done, at taxpayers' expense, in almost every community throughout our nation. Federal Community Action grants are flourishing to hire people to go out to count the number of poor, and ask these people why they are poor. "We haven't enough money" is not considered a good enough answer.

The Negro editor of the Pembroke Herald Eagle in Hopkins Park, Illinois, described all this nonsense this way:

"The evening of Monday July 26 marked a new foolish era of Pembroke Township . . . [which now] plans to hire an out-of-town stranger at $200 a week to tell Hopkins Park residents why they are poor . . .

"An OEO representative stated that this $30,000 [anti-poverty grant] must be spent by counting the number of people who live here, surveying the road conditions, and asking people why they are poor . . .

"Any fool walking or riding around Hopkins Park can see why the people are poor. They are poor because there is no payroll here . . . the problem is . . . not building day schools and clinics . . . this community needs a man that knows how to go out and bring business here."[13]

But for some reason no one seems to listen to such advice. The grants continue to roll out to organizations requesting the funds to "study" poverty, "count" the poor, and think up programs to spend more money on.

In Atascadero, California, an $18,000 poverty grant is being used to hire interviewers to go around asking the people why they are poor.[14] In commenting on how eager these people are to talk, one interviewer suggested a federal grant to hire people to go around and "just talk" to these people. Maybe what the program really needs is a good book of jokes.

We soon learned an important time saver in ploughing through the unending number of words in each Community Action report. First we turned to the budget and nine times out of ten, a large part of the real story was unfolded in these few pages. No ultra sophisticated lullabies here, but jazzy rock 'n roll aplenty.

Equipment is usually listed at the top retail price with no mention of possible quantity discounts (and certainly no mention of kick-backs). It is usually the finest available. Never just "typewriters," but always "electric typewriters." The reason offered, if and when anyone questions such luxuries, is that in the long run (and you can bet it's going to be a mighty long run) it pays to buy the best. If you can afford it, we agree. The problem is that after taxes, few of the less fortunate un-poor can afford it. Telephone and telegraph allowances for even the smallest of programs run $1,000 to $2,000 a year. Travel allowances ("intra and interstate" but don't ask us why) seem to have no limit. Executive desks at $350 each, new trucks, new filing cabinets, new everything.

A typical Community Action proposal usually states it intends to use donated space or backyards for the program, but in the budget column it is almost sure to request $10,000 or so to rent office space. Salaries always involve a director, assistant director, staff, and staff aides. Rarely are the "consultants" at so much (very much) a day forgotten, and the cost of evaluating the program never runs cheap. Usually there is something like a coordinator to coordinate the coordinators if the program is of any size at all.

The salaries of the *staff* of the Los Angeles anti-poverty agency (EYOA) represent close to a *million dollars annually*,* not to mention the salaries ($15,000 to $18,000)[15] of county and city "messenger boy" representatives. Since there were so many high salaried positions floating around, we asked a Los Angeles county official just who sets the salary scale. We were told by this anti-poverty official that salaries were scaled to recommendations from Governor Brown's State Personnel Board. This is fascinating when one considers that the President of this board is Joseph Wyatt, who is not only an active Democrat party man and past president of the California Democratic Council (CDC) but also the head of the Pasadena area anti-poverty agency and actively involved throughout the county in organizing War on Poverty groups.

No doubt each state has similar explanations for similar salary scales, so when you wonder why the director of the anti-poverty agency is receiving a higher salary than your elected mayor, or supervisor, just look a little deeper into the political power structure.

So it goes—the philosophy, that is. The government has the greater ability to pay more for less work with greater security. So unbeatable is the sales pitch, the federal government is buying itself deeper and deeper into a position of total control.

*A list of the full personnel obtained from the EYOA as of July 1, 1965 showed 5 employees at over $20,000 a year, 11 at over $15,000, 51 at over $10,000 and 87 at between $5,000 and $10,000. In addition, there are many sub-agencies throughout the county (Pasadena, Long Beach, etc.) which have their own paid (tax money) staff to work out programs before they are submitted to the Los Angeles anti-poverty agency.

Sometimes we ran into a program budget that appeared fair and reasonable (at least in comparison), only to discover that the request was funded, not on a year's expenditure, but for a period of four to six months. Or we found that salaries quoted involved only a piece of some professional's time.

However, it can get quite picayunish to quibble over a few thousand dollars here and there and everywhere when the over-all program is for such a "good" reason. After all, everyone hates poverty. We haven't quite decided who has the most twisted logic in determining a "good" cause. One proposal in Pasadena started out by way of explanation as follows:

"On August 13, 14, 15 and 16, 1965, a large number of young adult Negro males and females of the Northwest Pasadena community began the systematic sacking and looting of the North Fair Oaks area of the city of Pasadena . . .

"Feeling abused and short-changed in terms of life's chances, these young adults, about 125 in number" asked to meet with Negro professional business men of the community including representatives from the Council of Churches and the Pasadena School District.[16]

One could ask why, if these 125 adults "systematically sacked and looted" an area of Pasadena, they weren't arrested and put in jail. But to continue:

"As an outgrowth of these meetings (nine in number) the Northwest Pasadena Young Adult Project has emerged."

This good program for the 125 adults who systematically sacked and looted proposes to spend

$175,000 of the taxpayers' dollars as follows:

"Attend stage productions"

"Attend the Opera"

"Attend special sporting events"

"Attend concerts—classical and jazz"

"Dinners at middle class restaurants"

"Special non-group social events with girl and
boy friends"

"Rental of transportation"

"Lunch at work until payday (to be repaid—
we hope)"

"Securing legal aid and paying small traffic
court fines"[17]

The proposal goes on to explain that another project ("already in process") is the "expungement of police records (actions at law) so as to render the marginal young Negro adult employable."[18]

Although this program has just recently been submitted and has not been forwarded to Washington as yet, we use it because it so dramatically demonstrates the kind of things we can expect when the poor really take over direction of the War on Poverty.

Take, for instance, this business of erasing police records so as to "render the marginal young Negro employable." This has been recommended in many instances throughout the nation, from Rochester to Los Angeles, by militant Negro organizations.

The Los Angeles County Commission on Human Relations (headed by the John Buggs whom Saul Alinsky praised so highly for his skill in turning a tax supported commission into a militant organization) issued in November, 1965, a voluminous report on the Watts riots.

The report said it was "imperative that at least 5,000 jobs be made available within the next three weeks." It warned that "the tenor and tone of the community is ominous, and grows more so as promised jobs have not materialized."[19]

With the "either or else" gun subtly leveled at the rest of Los Angeles, the Human Relation's report goes on to a very carefully worded explanation of the "either" part of the warning:

"One of the problems faced in hiring persons from these areas, and especially the south Los Angeles area, is the fact that a large percentage of the population has a police record.

"At this time, the existence of a police record seriously limits the chances of an individual being hired by a public agency, or indeed, by many private businesses."[20]

The commission concludes that neither an arrest record nor a record involving criminal conviction should be used to deny a person the opportunity to work for a living.

Had the commission's wording been that police records should not "necessarily," be used to deny a person a job, the real meaning of what the commission appears to be saying would not be so apparent. The only way police records "can not be used," positively, is to erase them, isn't it?

In California, access to police records is denied by law to anyone other than law enforcement agencies.[21] However, court records (any action at law, including police action) are of public record. It is difficult, under these circumstances, to understand why these civil rights groups have directed their demands to "police records" rather than "court records," unless it is merely one more way of casting controversy on police departments.

It seems rather fundamental to us that any employer has the right to decide for himself if he wishes to take the calculated risk of hiring a person with a police record.

Actually the issue goes much deeper than just the employer's rights. Most judicious employers, and certainly all public agencies, require the bonding of employees who will be handling money or are in other positions of trust such as cashiers, clerks, truck drivers, warehousemen, etc. Before insuring a prospective employee, a private bonding company runs a routine check through credit records and court actions. Upon these records the risk (and possibly the cost) of bonding is decided.

War on Poverty officials have discovered that many of their trainees cannot be placed in jobs because they can not be bonded, the result being that the federal government becomes the bonding agent and agrees to pay all losses. The federal government, for paying purposes, being you.

If court records (police action) were to be erased or secreted, a monkey wrench would be thrown into the entire workings of bonding companies, which would no doubt mean that the government would take over the whole business of bonding, or the whole business of bonding would be eliminated. We can not determine whether the idea is for the government to pay the bonding charges through a private company, or to constitute itself as the bonding agency, for free.

We interviewed two men on this subject. One owns a bonding company and the other is head of a merchants' association. Both men said in substance, "Erasing of police records is absolutely ridiculous . . . we've never heard of such a thing . . . you must be mistaken . . . it just could never happen."

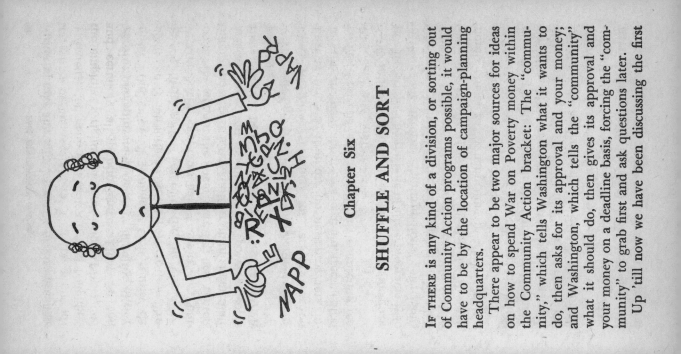

Chapter Six

SHUFFLE AND SORT

IF THERE is any kind of a division, or sorting out of Community Action programs possible, it would have to be by the location of campaign-planning headquarters.

There appear to be two major sources for ideas on how to spend War on Poverty money within the Community Action bracket: The "community," which tells Washington what it wants to do, then asks for its approval and your money; and Washington, which tells the "community" what it should do, then gives its approval and your money on a deadline basis, forcing the "community" to grab first and ask questions later.

Up 'till now we have been discussing the first

category, now let's take a look at the second. Some of the better known federal CAP programs are Head Start, Teenposts, Legal Aid, and Neighborhood Adult Participation Projects (NAPP).

Looking for a sort of federal backbone in their efforts to organize the poor into "effective political units," the Office of Economic Opportunity devised the Neighborhood Adult Participation Project (called NAPP if you're in the "in").

Most NAPP programs have "centers" or "outposts" throughout the poverty areas. These centers employ poverty stricken adults from the immediate area as "aides" on the theory that poverty people themselves can best help their neighbors solve their problems.

You will find NAPP aides on door-to-door canvasses recruiting members for various War on Poverty projects, thinking up new programs, informing the poor about free legal aid, free medical clinics, Project Head Start, family counseling services, and, and, and.

"Consumer Education" is one of the prime goals of this group. The purpose of these programs is to destroy (or reform) "unscrupulous" merchants who take advantage of the uninformed and undereducated indigent. This *sounds* great. But look at what the March, 1966, issue of *Nation's Business* points out as *really* happening in what it calls a tax financed "war on business":

"In the front window of a 'consumer education' office on a boulevard near the Capitol in Washington, tax-paid poverty fighters have plastered a handbill depicting the profit-bloated, horned caricature of a business leader in the act of snatching bread from the outstretched fingers of children.

"In Baltimore, poverty workers on the public payroll accompany housewives on shopping field trips, urging them to buy at large chain stores and pass up the small neighborhood markets they have traditionally patronized.

"In San Francisco, the director of a pilot project in consumer action freely concedes that 'consumer advisors' in his federally subsidized, $256,000 program get many of the buying hints they pass along to shoppers from cooperatives and the columns of the labor press. [BAND, which administers this project, has been accused of setting up merchandise co-operatives in direct competition with private enterprise.]

"Back in Washington, a high-spirited band of social workers, civil rights activists and others on the poverty payroll turned out on a workday recently to help the Student Nonviolent Co-ordinating Committee (SNCC) stage a city-wide boycott of the D.C. Transit Co. in protest against a proposed five cent fare increase. The boycott snarled traffic and cost the privately-owned bus facility an estimated 150,000 fares."

Leaving NAPP, we come to the neighborhood free-legal-service centers, which are just beginning to go into full operation.

Legal Aid is to many attorneys what Medicare is to many doctors. The federal government is now in the field of financing and providing legal services to the poor, who have always had free legal counsel in criminal cases and now will have it, at your expense, in civil cases. In essence this means that a taxpayer could find himself in the ridiculous position of paying the cost of a suit against himself.

According to California State legal consultant, James N. Reese, there will be no limit on the kind of cases the poverty funds will pay for and "suits could be filed against the federal government or the War on Poverty itself if the indigent had a case."[1]

Some attorneys feel that the possibility of federally financed attorneys going around stirring up law suits is a new approach to the law, and that the ethics of such activities is highly questionable.[2] Others feel that once this program really gets started it will smother out of existence the hundreds of competent local lawyers by the use of unlimited government funds, countless government lawyers, and innumerable government law offices established in whatever community they desire.[3]

The War on Poverty has grand aims in this legal aid field. An October, 1965, Allen-Scott report states, "They are talking of setting up a separate legal aid division, similar to the Job Corps, and financing it with a $20 million budget for the remaining eight months of the current fiscal year . . . the potential head of this proposed new division already has been brought in—Clinton Bamberger, Baltimore attorney."[4]

Guidelines for legal centers state that each center will maintain full time lawyers prepared to handle cases ranging from landlord-tenant disputes and domestic relations, to providing representation for the organizations of the poor such as credit unions, cooperatives, and community centers. Such representation may include helping the organizations to start, advising them concerning the organization's objectives (it helps to know, don't you think?), and representing them in litigation.

Again from the same Allen-Scott report:

"Nothing is said about politics—but it's a sure bet that won't be overlooked by the government-paid lawyers and sundry others!"

Two legal aid centers have been set up in Los Angeles to date. The total cost for just *operating* the two offices is $253,875 per year. As near as we can figure from their budget there is an overall director at $16,500, two directors for the offices at $14,000 each, and three attorneys for each office at from $800 to $1,000 per month.[5]

Three Negro attorneys have filed suit against the local Washington D.C. anti-poverty agency (United Planning Organization). They charge that the neighborhood free-legal-service centers are driving them out of business. The attorneys, Bruce Harrison, James Myrick, and Jerry Luck, realize they are taking on the power structure of Washington, but they say they are prepared to go all the way to the Supreme Court.

"We feel basic principles are being flouted and they must be upheld."[6]

Not only do they charge the activities of the center violate the anti-trust laws and ethical canons of the legal profession, but Mr. Harrison points out the definition of "poverty stricken" is wholly arbitrary:

"The current standard for free legal aid in Washington is $5,200 annual take-home pay for a family of four. This contrasts with the Labor Department's poverty standard of $3,000. But the Washington standard has never been consistent. There is nothing to prevent it from being raised to $7,200 . . . .

"I've spent 11 years building up a law practice. Now along comes this so-called anti-poverty program and sets up an indigency standard way above reason. It's destroying my business, and I don't propose to sit by and let them do that without fighting back."[7]

Move over, Mr. Harrison, a lot of us feel exactly the same way.

Chapter Seven

HEAD START

ONE of the more stylish federal performers in Community Action is "Head Start." Project Head Start, the pre-school program for little children from poverty areas, has had the largest build-up of any of the poverty programs, with the possible exception of the Job Corps. Head Start has also been the best received, possibly because little children are so sweet and innocent that only a Scrooge could oppose a program designed to help them.

But no matter how appealing the pictures of wide-eyed and eager children are, or how thick the coat of philanthropic goodness is, the fact remains that many of the same basic ills are flourishing in this program that abound in all of the other federally controlled programs.

Supposedly, this is an educational program, but nowhere is it required to be run by the local, or even the state educational facilities. Congressman Albert Quie led the Congressional opposition move to amend the law so as to correct this fault, but the Democrat majority refused to make the correction. Ask yourself *why*.

Any community action group can apply to the Office of Economic Opportunity for funds to hire teachers and conduct a pre-school nursery for poverty children. Apparently, such a group (an un-elected group) is not even required to submit a list of the names of those teaching in these classes. Neither the Office of Economic Opportunity nor community anti-poverty agencies require such a list. For all we (or they) know an illiterate but right-voting ex-convict could be hired as a teacher and even more likely as a teacher aide. Neighborhood Youth Corps (teenage school drop-outs) are frequently hired as "aides" . . . to set a good example for the wee ones?

Once more you are forced to pay the bill, but you have no control through your elected school board as to how, or for what, your money is being spent.

That the federal government is seeking central direction and control of education, was pointed out by Congressman Charles R. Jonas in July of 1965.[1] North Carolina already had 100 Head Start programs in operation, only they were called "Summer Readiness Programs" and involved no federal funds. The State was planning to increase these programs to 200 in 1965 and 300 in 1966. A request was submitted by the State education agency to the Office of Economic Opportunity to expand the program to 1,000 centers benefiting 15,000 children from poverty homes. The reply was:

"Community action programs are based on local communities . . . it is therefore not possible for us to approve a Head Start grant for North Carolina based on state administration of the funds and program."

Congressman Jonas stated that the North Carolina program costs $30 per child, as against a federal cost of $170 per child. "They were not interested in expanding a well established and efficiently operating program which would cost $140 per child less than the federal program but their concern was to retain control and direction of the program in the hands of federal officials," he commented.

It's not just a matter of getting a job done or the poor helped. *It makes a whale of a difference who is going to do the helping.*

With no fear of having to directly face the electorate, economy is seldom a major issue. Some nursery school teachers have reportedly been earning $200 a week for work in these day care Head Start centers.[2] In New York the salaries were reported at $9.20 an hour.[3] In Indiana teachers were recruited at salaries 25% above those paid in public schools.[4] Some Head Start expenses ran as much as $275 per pupil for eight weeks of the summer,[5] in communities where private nursery schools make money by charging about $75 for the same number of hours and even include hot lunches.

With words glowing in praise of the Great Society, Congressman James H. Scheuer (minimum income for everybody, remember?) reminded his colleagues in the House[6] that during the summer more than 400,000 part time volunteers had contributed to Head Start $90 million worth of time valued at $1.50 an hour. He reminded them that the Neighborhood Youth Corps and Neighborhood Adult Participation people had been "contributing" time in almost every one of these programs across the nation. (And may we remind you that these NYC and NAPP people are already on a federal anti-poverty payroll.) He said that many organizations have donated their services as well as buildings ... newspapers had given millions in free publicity.

All of this certainly appears to be a great testimonial to a great program.

But, just for fun, try adding all of these costs to an already costly program, then compare it with the cost of a profit making free-enterprise nursery school that has none of the volunteer services afforded Head Start. What conclusion do you get?

Juggling of statistics and language play a part in the true costs, too. For example, in Pasadena, the private school, Pacific Oaks College, received a $101,685 federal grant (plus $11,534 local cost) for their winter Head Start program.[7] Under "number to be served" they listed "1,000." Cost wise, this sounds within line. But when we read a bit more carefully into their proposal we discovered that the program was for only *120 pre-school children and their families*. Still farther on we found that many of the parents of these children were to receive salaries for their part in the program. For these 120 children, $92,000 was listed for personnel, of which only 8 were teachers. Out of a staff of 38, only four were paid on a full time basis. Most were listed at 1/5 time.[8]

The picture changes when the program is analyzed a bit below the surface. But then with the thousands of programs going direct to the Office of Economic Opportunity in Washington for approval, it would be unreasonable to expect that each program would be looked at in depth. Obviously the cost of checking on these expenditures would be fantastic, so there are those who reason that the taxpayer should shut up and not complain. At any rate, that's one way to go bankrupt. Every once in a while some fancy and almost humorous shenanigans are exposed. Senate investigators charged that a Mississippi minister who donated his church as a "free" Head Start headquarters was paid $100 rent for the use of a bathroom toilet for eight weeks. He was also said to have been paid $120 for the use of a refrigerator, $110 for a stove, $92 for a carpet and $10 for a garbage can.[9] But remember, he donated his church for "free," and after all how much do you expect for nothing?

Even Drew Pearson, who usually can swallow a whole herd of camels with a smile, reported that "doctors and dentists were paid a set fee for each child they examined for the Head Start program . . . some doctors rushed the exams so fast that they were able to collect $100 an hour."[10] How about that? Could this be a forecast of economy in federally financed Medicare?

While these particular doctors referred to by Mr. Pearson were obviously the "in" doctors, what about all the fine pediatricians who have agreed to donate their services? While educators, directors, and psychologists are getting paid fancy salaries, the services of these doctors are accepted as "tithing" to the Great Society.

This program has been accused of being the most expensive baby sitting program in our history. But in defense of such charges, and charges of high salaries, Congressman Sam M. Gibbons reminds us that teaching Head Start nurseries is "hard work . . . these children are given a lot more than just reading, writing, and arithmetic."[11] Former Congressman James Roosevelt urged the Negro community of Watts (prior to the riots) to remember that *their* children were forced to enter kindergarten not knowing how to even *read or write* . . . that they must DEMAND Head Start programs so that their children could at least start off on an equal footing with white children. The crowd of 1,000 Negroes loudly shouted their agreement.[12]

A Los Angeles group of Head Starters was taken to the very elegant Huntington Hartford Theater where some of the finest legitimate theater can be seen.[13] The Head Start director, overjoyed at the children's wide-eyed reaction, said, "Some of these children have never been to a theater [like this] before." Ever wonder how many five year olds have?

Republican Senators and Representatives have repeatedly charged that children of parents earning as much as $20,000 a year have frequently been enrolled in Head Start classes.[14] Congressman Adam Clayton Powell denied this, stating that the program was designed solely for children from poverty homes.[15] Despite this denial, children from non-poor and some-times very wealthy homes were and still are being enrolled in Head Start. Many areas are quite open about it, contending that the integration of poor and non-poor is good for both groups. Now that's a new cork in the integration bottle.

None of the application forms that we saw asked for family income information, or even mentioned that the program was designed for poverty-stricken families. Alaska reported Head Start wasn't even sold there as a poverty program.[16] In Pasadena the paper reported that any child coming from a home with an annual income of $3,000 or less could register, yet a few weeks later the Head Start director was quoted in the paper as saying, "We are able to welcome some children who will benefit from the program without restrictions as to family income."[17] Various doctors complained that they were giving free medical exams to children who were under the care of their family doctor or whose family had some form of medical insurance.[18] Congressman Charles E. Goodell said that his son Michael was invited to participate in the Head Start program for the District of Columbia, and asked, "Is this the intent of the bill—that children of Congressmen should be invited to participate in a Head Start program?"[19]

A federal Head Start grant of $1.4 million was given to a small Negro college in northern Mississippi. A Dr. Levin, from New York, came down to Mississippi, organized a child development group, and contracted with the college to set up 75 Head Start programs.* Dr. Levin said the policy of the child development group would be "aggressive compliance to the Civil Rights Act." He set up headquarters in a center called Mount Beulah in the small town of Edwards just outside Jackson. It was in this town that the massive Jackson demonstrations of the spring of 1965 were organized.

Describing this center as one that has been used by "pinks, punks and fellow travelers" for the past twenty years, Congressman John B. Williams goes on to explain that Mount Beulah is not only the headquarters for Head Start and VISTA, but also for the Council of Federated Organizations (COFO), the National Council of Churches, and the Freedom Democratic Party. It seems that even the phone numbers are the same. "If you can separate politics from that you're a wizard," the Congressman commented.

The next irregularity apparent in Mount Beulah's Head Start venture was the charge by a Negro college graduate and teacher that she had not been given a job in Head Start because she had not

*The Mount Beulah story as we recount it has been paraphrased from the account given in the Congressional Record, July 21, 1965, pp. 16985-87.

been active in the civil rights movement. Her charge was substantiated by the fact that others with fewer qualifications, but more active politically, were hired, and by the fact that the questionnaire submitted to those seeking a position asked "What has been your experience in the civil rights movement?"

Upon repeated Congressional demands, Sargent Shriver finally released the information that qualifications are not based upon civil rights participation, and that the man doing the interviewing, a Mr. Fawcett, was not on the federal payroll. But what Mr. Fawcett was doing there in the first place, making and taking these applications and hiring and firing these people, and *whose* payroll he was on, was never disclosed.

According to Congressman Williams, Myles Horton, an "avowed socialist and communist sympathizer who ran what has been described as a Communist training school in Tennessee" has been seen frequently at the center. Also Carl and Ann Braden, "both notorious communists," have been operating in and out of Mount Beulah for quite some time.

From this background the pre-school for little children began.

The first day of the Mount Beulah Head Start "classes" revealed to a reporter from the Clarion Ledger (Jackson) that at one center where eight adults were present, six were known COFO and SNCC workers who had participated in demonstrations. Three of the six were known to have had specific trouble with the law. One had been arrested for assault and battery when she hit a Greenwood policeman. Another had been arrested in Jackson the preceding month. The third had listed herself as a "pacifist and tax refuser" when she was hired! When questioned about such people serving as

Head Start teachers, a spokesman said they were well aware of it, thank you, and that in most cases such people were the community leaders.

One of the advantages these little five year olds will receive from your tax dollars is an early introduction to the needed qualifications for community leadership, like hitting policemen, serving a jail sentence, and being a "tax refuser."

Now that summer is over and the program is continuing into the fall it has been disclosed that Mount Beulah anti-poverty officials squandered $20,000 earmarked for food, overpaid a New York accounting firm $12,500, and used federal Head Start funds to bail out arrested civil rights workers.[20]

Although these examples and many more can't be dismissed as "isolated cases," nevertheless Head Start has not always been filled with greedy opportunists. Many programs, of course, have been conducted by sincere (but possibly naive) people eager to help break the deploring cycle of poverty acquiescence by working through the very young. But we feel the "means" just might be justifying a completely different "end" than these dedicated people have in mind.

On the other hand, there are those who question the whole value of Head Start programs for the poor. "The Failure of a Nursery School Enrichment Program for Culturally Disadvantaged Children" is the lengthy title of a report by Dr. Gerald D. Alpern, Director of Research, Child Psychiatry Services, Indiana University Medical School. It recounts the findings from a series of tests involving poverty children who had preschool training and those who had not. There was no evidence found in these tests that pre-school training "could significantly alter" the attitudes and learning characteristics of "lower-class children."

"The intelligence of the children was unaffected . . .

"In none of the comparisons of verbal skills, information and school readiness were there any significant differences between the group that attended the nursery school and the group which did not attend . . .

"The results of the study to date are concluded to bring into serious question assumptions concerning the benefits to poverty stricken children of a nursery school enrichment program . . . at this point, we count ourselves a deeply skeptical group."[21]

The federal government reports that it enrolled 561,000 youngsters during the summer at a cost of $83 million. It is spending $150 million for the fall and winter Head Start program.[22]

Head Start is now a year round program. It has a follow up program that continues into the regular grades of school, so it no longer is just a pre-school deal.[23] We are told that there is a plan under consideration to make this whole program compulsory for the deprived child. Who decides which child is deprived? Remember, this is a federally financed program which can be run by unelected, virtually self-appointed people.

We are not qualified to make a sound judgment on whether Head Start can or can not provide a significant step forward for poverty children, but we can make a sound prediction as to the inevitable results of turning over the education of our children to the federal government.

Chapter Eight

THE TEENPOST TWIST

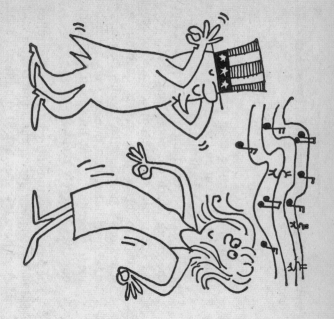

THERE is no question about the roaring success of one phase of the federally thought-up Community Action programs, at least in the opinion of the participants. Teenposts have been so popular with teenagers that practically everyone has jumped on the bandwagon in support of these federally financed youth clubs.

It is not difficult to understand the reason teenagers loudly acclaim the popularity of their posts, or centers, or clubs, or whatever you choose to call them. What Los Angeles teenager wouldn't like free trips to Disneyland, Marineland, Knott's Berry Farm, and even to San Francisco? Who among us wouldn't like to attend dances, go on pack trips to the high Sierras, and have evenings at fancy theaters with all expenses paid?[1] And then what about the joyous job of a Neighborhood Youth Corps enrollee who is employed as a "Teenpost Aide" at $1.27 an hour?

How lucky can you get?

Trying to be objective about all of this, we had to admit that any teenager with all his marbles would be enthusiastic when all these things were handed to him on a specially designed silver platter. The teenagers to whom this platter is passed not only do not have to work for what they get," they are not even expected to say "thank you." These young people are being taught, not generally but specifically if you please, that all of this is not one whit more than their due. This is so-ciety's obligation to them . . . because they are poor.

When this program was first proposed in the Los Angeles area, TAXACTION, Inc., a large and ac-tive taxpayers' organization, decided to take a penetrating look at the situation. In early June of 1965 the Teenpost proposal was praised in article after article in the Los Angeles Times as being ab-solutely essential if we were to avoid a "long hot summer of racial strife." A large front page pic-ture was set up depicting teenagers standing on a street corner . . . "bored and idle."[2] This constant quoting of the typical teenager from poverty areas as "having nothing to do" piqued the curiosity of this taxpayers group. Some members wondered out loud if perhaps the local taxpayer had really fallen down on the job.

So TAXACTION made a survey of what was presently available for these poverty area teenagers. From the Los Angeles City Department of Recre-ation, a study committee learned exactly what programs were available, close by, and without charge. The result was a list of programs that took *50 feet* of shelf paper to list!

Hundreds of programs including free lessons in every sport imaginable . . . dances . . . clubs . . . crafts . . . camping . . . excursions . . . trips to museums, zoos, and Knott's Berry Farm . . . opportunities to volunteer as assistants and leaders in programs for younger children ending in a trip as a reward . . . the list appeared endless, the facilities were amazing, and opportunities for fun and rewarding self-improvement were unbelievable. All free and all at local taxpayers expense . . . all 50 feet.

TAXACTION pointed out that this long list did *not* include programs sponsored by the tax supported city schools such as a complete recreational program of their own, along with, of course, summer school with its free courses in typing, reading, math, science, homemaking, and dozens of other subjects. Nor did it include the programs of voluntary agencies such as the YMCA, YWCA, Boy's Clubs, Girl's Clubs, Boy Scouts, Girl Scouts, Camp Fire Girls, and the many other fine youth organizations supported by volunteer giving. It also omitted all of the programs and campership funds sponsored by civic organizations. Finally, the list omitted the many programs offered by almost every neighborhood church organization. The 50 foot list was *only* what local taxes provided, and only part of that.

Yet according to the protagonists of this Teenpost program, these young people had nothing to do but be "bored and idle." Hearing it repeated over and over on television, in the papers, and in neighborhood meetings, the teenager soon was convinced his life was a bottomless pit of boredom. Billed as a program "of the teens, by the teens, and for the teens" and conceived as a means of "keeping otherwise idle youngsters busy during the hot summer months," the money for 120 teenposts came through in the infamous summer of 1965.

Mrs. Fifi Boger, coordinator of the program, explained that *existing* programs were something like a stigma to these youngsters who "wouldn't be caught dead in some of them." Teenposts, she explained, "give them a location of their own . . . and they don't have policy imposed from above. They'll determine their own conduct and set their own restrictions."3

After you have re-read that quote a couple of times and jumped to a few hysterical conclusions, backup and give Mrs. Boger credit for having hit the nail on the head. According to Department of Recreation authorities their programs which compete with the Teenposts are not as popular as they would like because to placate nasty old public opinion they *do* have to set and enforce certain standards of behavior. Teenagers, for example, are even forbidden to take alcoholic refreshment. Compare that with Teenpost policy of letting teenagers "determine their own conduct and set their own restrictions."

This they obviously did at a War on Poverty youth club in Venice, California. According to reports in the September 20, 1965, Santa Monica Evening Outlook:

"Neighbors complain that loud music, raucous arguing and noisy drinking bouts are keeping them awake . . . until early morning hours and nearly everyday leave a litter of empty bottles outside."

These charges were countered by the director of the Venice post, Mr. Frank Eydent. He said the purpose of the program was "to rehabilitate teenagers, high school dropouts, and young adults." He went on to explain that:

> ". . . if you're only going to stay open until 9:30 you might as well close up . . . sure you have drinking sometimes, but you have to remember that the age of some of our members runs as high as 35 years. I've never seen a teenage dance in a poverty area where there hasn't been drinking."[4]

So according to schoolteacher Eydent, it is better for these teenagers, poverty-stricken and sometimes supposedly hungry, to get drunk at a tax-supported youth club (that has 35-year-old members) than someplace where they might get picked up by the police, such action no doubt resulting in all sorts of damage to their psychological well-being. If, in your own home, you were to allow such activities, you probably would be arrested for contributing to the delinquency of minors. But then, your parties are not trying to rehabilitate a teenager by letting him determine his own conduct and set his own restrictions.

Teenposts have now been extended on a year round basis so as to provide an outlet for teenagers not only in the summer but also in after school hours and during the weekends. Any reader who has recently gone through the grueling experience of his child's high school homework routine just *has* to wonder about all this teenage need for recreation in after school hours. Parents of modern teenagers long ago gave up the theory of "family togetherness" during the school week . . . there is never time for it.

Could it be that these particular teenagers are not required to do any homework? Are they just passed from one grade to the next without complying to the standards required of others? Could this be why the Job Corps is getting 10th and 11th grade drop-outs who can't pass a 4th grade curriculum test?

The Los Angeles Times carried a story on the War on Poverty in which the hunger and boredom of Negro teenagers were discussed.[5] A teenage girl was quoted as saying she was wasting her time going to school. "After two months of this," she said in reference to a particular class, "there wasn't nuthin' else to do so I might as well come to school drunk—I quit."

The obvious questions to all but the liberal sociologists and the Los Angeles Times are: Where did she get the money to get "drunk," why did she not buy food instead of liquor, and why wasn't she expelled instead of "dropping out?" * Can you imagine what would happen if your child arrived at school just *one* morning drunk?

The cost of the proposed 200 Teenposts in Los Angeles was budgeted in the fall at $4.8 million.[6] With one of its rare glances at costs, the Los Angeles anti-poverty board (EYOA), decided that, worthy as the Teenposts were, it couldn't allocate 4.8 million to them in view of the many other "worthy" programs still to be financed. The board agreed to approve 100 Teenposts at a cost of close to three million dollars. Each post was to have a director, two adult aides, four teenage aides, *and* its own individual budget of $28,000 for eight months of operational costs. The project's general budget included "$160,000 for consultant and contract services, $88,000 for travel, $200,000 for space costs and rentals, $400,000 for supplies,

*The American Civil Liberties Union was so impressed with the approach that the Los Angeles Times took in this series of articles, "A View from Watts," that it awarded the Times author, Jack Jones, with a $500 token of their appreciation.[7]

$80,000 for equipment, and $258,000 for other expenses."[8]

We can think of nothing that would have prompted half the storm that erupted. Teenagers came in droves from the Watts area to demonstrate to the board their desire for more, not fewer, Teenposts. But believe it or not, the board did not submit this time to the pressure. The decision remained to hold at just 100 posts.[9]

The following week one board representative from the poverty area meekly voiced a protest. It seemed that during the preceding week he had attended neighborhood meetings at which teenagers had booed, hissed, and spit because of the action he, as a member of the EYOA, had taken in regards to the Teenposts. He suggested to the director of the Teenpost project, present at this board meeting, that perhaps more effort could be made to explain to the kids that the board was only trying to do what it felt best for *all* concerned, that the board simply couldn't afford everything on the money said to be allotted to it from Washington, and that the behavior of these teenagers was not in "very good taste."[10]

The director said she realized this but that these youngsters wanted these posts so very much it was impossible for them to understand why they couldn't have them, and it did seem to her that when a program had proven as popular as this one that some priority should be given to it. However she wanted it understood that she could not control what these children thought or did.

Another member of the board, Irvin Mazzei (AFL-CIO representative on EYOA), was less timid in his concern of the behavior of these "children." He said that he was "no hero" and implied that he wanted out, out, out. Three phone calls threatening his life may have figured in his statement. Teenposts just weren't *that* important to him. At the first mention of the phone calls, a startled but quick-witted board member quickly moved the board into executive session and the room was cleared of all spectators and press, thus sparing Mr. Massei from the embarrassment of any further airing of his sensibilities. But the kitty was out of the bag.[12]

Today's teenagers need "understanding." And when you understand a teenager, you jolly well give him what he wants, when he wants it. So say the sociologists, and they get paid to know.

Chapter Nine

SELF EXPRESSION IN THE JOB CORPS

BRAWLING, drinking, knifing, killing, sexual assaults, rioting, narcotics, extortion. These are the words heading news stories on the federal Job Corps centers throughout the country. It's not a pretty picture, and those words don't begin to tell the whole sordid story. That this particular caliber of young people are involved in such orgies is no real surprise; the real shocker is the attitude, explanations, and excuses emanating from Washington. And the cost . . . wow!

The Job Corps, first of all, is not a job corps. It offers no jobs nor even any guarantee of a job. It is a program in which young people who have dropped out of school, who are unemployed, and who allegedly come from poverty-stricken homes can sign up for a stint in a rural and/or urban training center (reminiscent of F.D.R.'s CCC camps). Basic work programs and remedial education are supposedly the major tools used to train these young adults to take a more productive role in society. But don't be surprised to find some other kind of tools being used to do something or other.

Each corpsman is given free food and lodging, and supplied with uniform blue blazers and grey trousers.[1] Besides being transported to and from the center (as far from his home as possible), he is paid about $80 per month* plus $50 per month payable on termination.[4] If $25 of this $50 is sent home each month the government matches it with an additional $25 to the home.[5] He is given around $75 for purchasing clothes of his choice. He is given all of his health expenses. He is given free legal aid to protect his rights should he feel he is being mistreated and to defend him if he gets in trouble.

At Christmas time he is given a fully paid 10 day "leave" to go home. There are Job Corps officials at the departure and arrival airports, bus and railroad terminals "to help those who get lost or confused," as well as "at least one" official "at home" visit during the holidays just to make sure everything is going along all right.[6] Or is it just to make sure the enrollee comes back to camp? Regardless ... can it justify the exorbitant cost?

The cost per year to train each corpsman averages somewhere between $5,000 and $6,000.[7] Compare this with an accepted average cost of one year

*The Economic Opportunity Act leaves the exact amount of living and travel allowances to the "discretion of the director." Sargent Shriver reports $30 per month is the going rate[2] but various Congressmen and newsmen report monthly allowances ranging from $30 to $200 per month.[3]

of college at $2,500 to $3,500 including food and lodging, books, and personal expenses.[8]

In January, 1965, communities across the nation began voicing their fear of incurring additional community problems by the establishment of these nearby Job Corps camps and bringing in of delinquents from Harlem and elsewhere. They were repeatedly assured by top officials that these camps would not be filled with young punks, that members were to be carefully screened and supervised:[9]

"A screening process has been set up to find those young men and women who, though uneducated and unskilled, have the basic minimum requirements of aptitude, health and ambition that will enable them to break the bonds of poverty.

"The Job Corps is neither a sanitarium for incurables nor a correctional institute for incorrigibles. Nor is it simply a breadline."

Congressional Presentation,
Office of Economic Opportunity,
April, 1965

These carefully screened and supervised Job-corpsmen have been busy proving that if these statements are not ridiculous, then a new definition of "punk" and "incorrigible" is in order. Excerpts from a few stories picked up by the press will make the point:

Redding, California: June, 1965
Citizens demand action be taken about the lack of discipline in the nearby Lewiston Job Corps camp. Cited are examples of one corpsman knifing another, of a wild shooting spree in a Redding parking lot, and charges by merchants that adult corpsmen were buying liquor and providing it to camp minors.[10]

San Antonio, Texas: July, 1965

Two Camp Gary job corpsmen were charged with robbery and attempted murder. The gun was found in the bus hired to take the trainees back to camp after a Saturday night in town.[11]

Poughkeepsie, New York: July, 1965

Police staged an early morning raid on a nearby Job Corps camp and arrested eight enrollees on charges ranging from possession of narcotics to possession of deadly weapons.[12]

St. Petersburg, Florida: July, 1965

A woman's Job Corps center located in a neighborhood of hotels and apartments primarily for retired people caused a scandal that shook both houses of Congress during their debates on the Poverty Program. Girls were reported soliciting, drunk, pregnant, and with their rock and roll, hot-rod boy friends, were causing the ruination of the up-to-then respectable neighborhood. The scandal was not limited to the behavior of the girls. The "country club" staff was listed at 122 (drawing $56,843 monthly) to serve 222 girls. On the staff of a camp center that had no swimming pool was a full time swimming instructor at $8,160 and a full time life guard at $6,000! Although detailed medical examinations were given by outside doctors, a part time medical director was employed at $1,000 a month. The federal government had leased the Job Corps hotel for 18 months at $20,000 more than the hotel's total appraised value.[13]

Morganfield County, Kentucky:
August, 1965

Camp Breckinridge Urban Job Corps center was the scene of a full scale riot involving over 150, and injuring 10. The FBI came to the rescue because state police and local authorities had no jurisdiction on federally owned land. Charles Preston, in charge of public relations for the camp, said that the riot had racial overtones, that it was not a spontaneous affair, and that causes ranged from charges of extortion (requiring corpsmen to pay $13.50 a month for "life insurance") to complaints that the food was "slop." Mr. Preston said, "The students were fighting everybody—themselves and the camp officials. They grabbed everything they could get their hands on and went wild." Almost 200 youths were forced to flee and were put up in nearby hotels . . . the taxpayer, of course, picked up the tab. Prior to the riot Camp Breckinridge had been picketed by the NAACP claiming discrimination and stirring up racial unrest.[14]

Two months later:

The $10 million Job Corps center at Camp Breckinridge was again hit with trouble when it was disclosed that the director's wife and the wives of 51 other employees were on the camp's payroll. These wives were among the 107 fired, which brought the staff of Camp Breckinridge *down to 350 for a reported 358 trainees.*[15]

Kalamazoo, Michigan: November, 1965

More than 100 youths led by trainees from nearby Fort Custer Job Corps center rampaged through downtown Kalamazoo fighting police, smashing store windows and looting.

(Our note: What about your child in a public school classroom with only one teacher for 30 to 35 students? This camp had virtually a one to one ratio.)

Witnesses said youths smashed policemen with bottles and tried to stab one. About 100 policemen helped by citizen volunteers battled the youths and finally broke up the melee only after the mob had torn through seven downtown blocks. The fight erupted at a school dance to which the job corpsmen had been invited.[16]

Mountain Home, Idaho: November, 1965

Paul Dennis Jones, a California youth on parole after three felony convictions, beat and stabbed a fellow corpsman at the Mountain Home Job Corps Center in Idaho. He was in violation of his parole at the time. Job Corps officials reportedly refused to cooperate with the local prosecuting attorney, but they paid for an attorney and psychiatric treatment for the 20-year old defendant. Congressmen Charles Goodell and Albert Quie said that Jones was a dormitory leader, wing leader and squadron leader at the time of his arrest, despite his criminal record. They said a telegram from Washington asked that Jones be returned to the center without punishment, but the judge sentenced him to a four-month term after which the Job Corps agreed to take him back.[17]

Omaha, Nebraska: December, 1965

The women's Job Corps Center in Omaha has been involved in such ventures as flying enrollees to work at the New York World's Fair and at a Gemini launching at the Houston (Texas) space center. The Omaha Evening World Herald says: "Omaha area school districts couldn't afford to send their most promising science students to Gemini launch, but taxpayers' money was available to send corps girls there even though they aren't interested in careers in the space program." Costs in this center are run up by frequent flying visits from federal officials and paid consultants, for searchers for runaways, for chaperones to escort girls on out-of-town trips, for renovation of leased buildings, medical checkups, hair grooming and monthly allowances which surpass a fighting G.I.'s pay.[18]

Camp Atterbury, Indiana:
November, 1965

Congressman Richard Roudebush has requested the closing of the $10 million Job Corps camp at Camp Atterbury, charging that it is costing the taxpayers about *$22,000 per corpsman.*[19] Surrounding community townsfolk have been continuously harassed by unruly corpsmen. In words quoted by a former Job Corps counselor at the camp, the philosophy at these camps is "spoil these boys—they have never been spoiled before." The predictable result was summed up by the Indianapolis News: "Gangs were organized. Fights between corpsmen . . . were frequent. Smaller, weaker corpsmen became the targets of ruffians who operated protection rackets. One report said corpsmen who couldn't pay protection were either beaten or sexually assaulted. The assault sometimes took the-form of gang rapes."[20] Trainees have been arrested on charges ranging from sodomy, to assault, to drunkenness. Recently 30 members were invited to an evening's entertainment at the town's auto raceway. The job corpsmen showed their appreciation by shouting obscenities and creating a small scale riot. Christopher Weeks, then Deputy Job Corps Director in Washington, explained away the "incident" by *blaming the citizens of Atterbury*:

"Many job corpsmen feel they are not welcome in the communities adjacent to Atterbury . . . if they are rejected, they react accordingly—and who can blame them?"[21]

We'll ask the wacky question again. Who can blame these "well screened and supervised" youngsters for rioting when they feel rejected?

How many hands are raised?

This program is so permeated with destructive approaches and politics that even the location of these Job Corps centers is beginning to take a political turn. For example, in Bismarck, North Dakota, Mayor Evan Lips insisted that his city strenuously objected to having a Job Corps center. The wishes of this Republican community have been ignored.[22] Yet when Minneapolis, Hubert-Humphreyland, objected to a woman's job corps in their city, the powers that be looked for a site elsewhere.

Despite the Job Corps being launched with a publicity spree of propaganda that should have made the taxpayer howl with outrage, the Job Corps has run into nothing but problems from the very beginning. Quotas have not been filled. Drop-out rates have been alarming, especially when one thinks of just the cost of processing applications and providing transportation across the country and then back again when the enrollee decides after a few weeks he's had enough and wants to go home. Drop-out percentages ran from 20% to 50% depending upon whose figures were used. Explanations varied from "homesickness" to "misunderstandings." In interviews with job corpsmen, some of whom were quitting and going home, it was found that many felt they could get a better education at night school back home, some said they were sorry they had quit their jobs to join the Job Corps (!), and almost all complained that the work at camp wasn't what was pictured to them back home.

Film strips, pamphlets, even T.V., have been used by the Office of Economic Opportunity to picture camps in which enrollees are happily working with large equipment. In reality work consists mainly of routine labor and remedial education courses, with a considered emphasis on recreational programs.

Word got out that many recruiting centers were being paid $80 per each accepted Job Corps enrollee they could recruit. Senator Peter Dominick said, "Here we are operating almost like a slave market, paying $80 a head to shanghai people to the Job Corps. I can hardly conceive of anything like this going on."[23] With some 1700 screening centers[24] across the nation, many enthused by the financial rewards and most under political pressure to enroll as many as possible, the tendency has been (aided and abetted by the Office of Economic Opportunity) to over-glamorize life at Job Corps camps. Pictures show food served to overflowing from breakfast and dinner trays.

"What'll we have for breakfast this morning?" a film strip voice asks in a cheerful, hand-rubbing way. "French toast? Bacon and eggs? Go on, help yourself. There's more where that came from."[25]

So, when D-6, 7, 8, or 9 tractors are not given to them to operate, when possibly they aren't given a choice between French toast or eggs, or at the first sign of adult chastisement or neighborhood criticism, they go on a destruction rampage or demand a return ticket home (and get it).

If there is one basic thing that is all wrong, it is the one sentence in the current camp instructions which reads, "Formal disciplines must be kept to a minimum."[26]

Job Corpsmen are tough, unmanageable teen-agers, for the most part, from slums and broken homes. They are desperately in need of discipline . . . for someone who cares enough to teach them the benefits of discipline. But apparently it must be kept to a "minimum" for fear of "frightening" them off.

A camp official at the Pleasanton, California Job Corps center said:

"Conscious effort has been made to de-emphasize military aspects of the training . . . we are trying to get away from army terms so we don't scare the kids."[27]

(Who's scaring whom?)

Floating around now is an argument that the disadvantaged backgrounds of these Job Corps volunteers entitle them to unique advantages when they reach camp. The prevailing theory is that these youths must be given an exposure to a grandiose way of life they supposedly never even dreamed existed before. Since most of *our* grandiose living has been of the vicarious variety, we're not sure what this is supposed to accomplish other than envy and resentment when it no longer is being given to them.

Pasadena's famous New Year's Rose Parade and Rose Bowl Game were chosen as the scene for one of these cultural exposure trips. As a prize for the winners of a national Job Corps "Punt, Pass and Kicking" contest—boys from various centers across the nation were given a New Year's trip to Pasadena. The recreation director accompanying them told us they were "having the best of everything." They went to the finest restaurants the area offered during these days of wine and roses. All they had to do was hand the restaurant owner a meal voucher which the owner then had to send to Washington in order to get paid for the $4.50 steak dinners[28] that had been served.

The typical confusion prevalent throughout all of the War on Poverty activities flared into misunderstandings over which boys from which camps should drink of the culture afforded by a trip to the City of Roses. A director of the Fenner Canyon Job Corps camp in Los Angeles county was openly upset that his boys had at first been offered the opportunity to participate in the festivities, and then the offer, for unknown "political reasons" according to him, was withdrawn.

When we talked with this director he knew nothing about any contest for punting, passing, and kicking . . . which makes one wonder *which* camps did.

This director went on to explain to us that he felt unless drastic changes were made, the entire program would continue to be the dismal failure it presently is. He feels that these boys are not getting the finest of everything—which they "*must*" —and he pointed out that the Fenner Canyon center had no recreation hall, no gym, none of the essential recreational facilities needed to make these boys happy. He asked if we could believe it possible that the only long trip the camp had sponsored in eight months was a trip to the Grand Canyon and *Las Vegas*. We responded with words of honest shock which he interpreted to his satisfaction. We didn't dare ask what Las Vegas had to do with the supposed purpose of the Job Corps . . . but it probably had the same something-to-do-with-it that $1,350 had when it was used to hire the Ink Spots and other high priced rock 'n roll groups to entertain the boys at Camp Atterbury.[29]

Along this same line of thinking, Rutgers University was hired to do a thorough study of Camp Kilmer Urban Job Corps center in New Jersey. This center has been billed as a War on Poverty "show case." In the bitterly critical study, the Rutgers professors argued that the camp management was interfering with the normal personality patterns of the boys! Entrance procedures were described as "a series of degradations, humiliations and profanations of self." The professors went on to:

"The corpsman loses his identity equipment, whether it be black leather jackets, long hair, narrow pants, or whatever. These gave the individual a sense of his usual image of himself to others. To be stripped of them, no matter how well intended the stripping, is an egregious action against the corpsmen."[30]

(Why not read that professorial statement again!)

The professors went on to urge removal of the fences around the camp, more pay for the corpsmen, more recreation, transportation into New York for the theater, "soft drink night club rooms" and a coffee house on the base, radios in every room, and a complete reversal of the "paramilitary" atmosphere and the "authoritarian" attitude of the staff.

Charles Bartlett, in his December 3, 1965, syndicated column, sums up the Rutgers report by saying that it is clear that the professors have in mind a sort of "Disneyland for the Disadvantaged." He feels that a great weakness of the camp, as it is now operated, is the heavy emphasis on fun and recreation which is judged necessary to keep the boys in camp.

"The slum-like accumulation of trash and paper that litters the grounds is depressing testimony to the fact that the camp's discipline has a narrow focus. Even more depressing is the mess hall where hired janitors sweep up the bread, napkins, and silverware which are strewn about the floor during every meal."

Discipline is required of men fighting and dying for their country. Education is required to the age of 16. If these Job Corps boys are ever going to hold an honest job they will have to learn to take orders. Are there really any valid reasons why these teenagers, who are being supported by your dollars, should not be required to study, to accept rules, and to stick out a prescribed course? The kid glove treatment, "Please, don't you want to come and try to improve yourself?", is not only out of character, considering the past performance of the very majority of these teenagers, but also ignores the very concept that will be the most meaningful to them in the work-a-day life which we might hope is ahead of them. That concept is simply that the ability to accept discipline is basic to earning a living.* The outlandish cost of these camps is exceeded only by the outlandish philosophy perpetrated.

One last parting question before we leave the Job Corps to its problems and our money: Where have the rewards for being good gone? One of the

*According to the Los Angeles Times (May 6, 1965) one of the "architects" of the Job Corps in California was Paul Jacobs who was identified in the same story as one of the leaders who instigated demonstrations at the University of California against the President's foreign policy. "We resign from the horrible war!" he declared in presenting a pacifist manifesto signed by 50-some California University professors. Later that same day, according to columnist Holmes Alexander in the August 24 Berkeley Gazette, 40 students held a rally and publicly burned their draft cards.

most ridiculous aspects of this program was pointed out on the floor of the Senate last August by Senator Peter Dominick.[31] Take, for example, two brothers, he said. One brother finishes first in his class at high school, has conformed to the laws of society, and is eager to forge ahead in education and a profession. We reward him by dressing him in khaki, paying him $78 a month, and ordering him to Viet Nam to risk his life for his country. His brother, who has another set of values, beats up his mother and his teachers, drops out of school, and joins the Job Corps. We dress him in a blue blazer and gray slacks, pay him more than his brother, and "ask" him if he'd mind doing a little studying and perhaps rake a few leaves . . . if it isn't too much to ask, that is.

Chapter Ten

THE NEIGHBORLY THING TO DO

Don't confuse the Neighborhood Youth Corps (NYC) with the Job Corps. They are two completely different programs. Perhaps the easiest way to keep them distinct is to remember that the Job Corps is conducted in centers and camps far, far away from home, whereas the Neighborhood Youth Corps is a *neighborhood* program which does not involve going away somewhere to live.

Secretary of Labor, Willard Wirtz (boss man of NYC), announced that, "The primary goal of the Neighborhood Youth Corps is to provide the necessary income to our young people so they can remain in or return to school."[1] As usual, the stated goal and the actual facts differ!

The NYC program involves both in-school and out-of-school young people from low income families. It provides that they may be employed by public agencies, such as the schools and city government agencies, or by private non-profit organizations, such as the YWCA, United Way, or any non-profit group. Supposedly the jobs are to "increase their employability or enable the resumption or continuation of their education."[2] The federal government will pay $1.27 to $1.44 an hour[3] for such jobs as library aides, gardener trainees, garage attendants, playground attendants, etc., provided that these jobs "will not result in the displacement of employed workers or impair existing contracts for services."[4]

The hourly wage scale for these jobs was originally a hot issue nationally. Union leaders railed at "social workers" who, they claimed, would set up youth employment programs with low wage scales without seeking labor's views on the matter. "If we're not consulted on a program, we'll knock its damn ears off," fumed a Mr. Sullivan of the Boston Labor Council.[5] George Meany, President of the AFL-CIO, and other union leaders insisted that NYCers be paid at least $1.25 an hour, and poverty officials bowed to their demands.[6]

But there have been some interesting wage scale maneuvers prevalent in the NYC regulations, and Senator Peter Dominick was bitterly critical last August of such practices:

"If it [NYC] is designed to help the children continue their education, it is difficult for me to see why jobs should be made on campuses by way of picking up sticks, which is a part of the program, or cleaning latrines, which is another part of it, and paying them a dollar and a quarter an hour, as requested by the Department of Labor, and then requiring the schools to falsify their records submitted to the Government . . .

"What they say now is, 'You must pay $1.25 an hour for the work they are doing, but when you publicize what you are doing, include within it the number of hours when they are actually training and not being paid for work, and then you will reduce the total pay, so that it will come down to about 90 cents an hour, which is what you are paying ordinarily, and then you will not be driving out the people hired at that level.'

"I think it is plainly deceitful, and I said so."[7]

Poverty officials are quick to explain that none of these NYC jobs jeopardize an unemployed adult's chances for a job. Consequently, it must be that these NYC jobs are non-essential . . . sort of a make-work variety. Such jobs as raking leaves, cleaning blackboards, and parking cars are typical. Often it is just standing around waiting for a well paid employee to show them what to try to do, which seldom impresses either employee or trainee. Sometimes the make-work jobs are just plain ludicrous.

In Livingston County, Illinois, an NYC employee was hired to announce scores of Little League games. Another was given a job assisting the manager of a Little League team who was serving without pay. Others were hired to pull grass from sidewalk cracks.[8] An enthusiastic city official in Chattanooga, Tennessee, hired two high school drop-outs to work in the public library to compile a bibliography, only to find to his some-time-later dismay that the teenagers couldn't read![9]

The uncomfortable mistake of hiring illiterates to work in a public library is bad enough, but the NYC has hit more serious problems than that. Despite generous allocations of tax funds for NYC salaries to schools, cities, and organizations, job openings are just not being filled. Headlines in local newspapers across the nation read "Jobs Go Begging," or "Jobs Galore for the Taking." In Riverside, California, after the NYC placement officer and his staff had visited 70 high schools and junior colleges and mailed information to as many more, only 30 out of 209 positions were filled.[10]

In Detroit, Michigan, only 800 out of an anticipated 1500 youths took advantage of job opportunities, despite agency recruiters "canvassing," the streets. It seems many of the youths refused to work for the standard $1.25 an hour. Recruiters heard responses such as, "You're crazy man, I don't work for that kind of money."[11]

In Pasadena, California, the city's Junior College has a campus employment office. This office reported that 20-25 jobs a week are turned down because, among other things, students consider such jobs as gardening to be "dirty."[12] Despite this, the school board, acting upon the recommendation of Superintendent Robert E. Jenkins, entered into a college NYC program to use taxpayers' money to pay these students $1.40 an hour to do work that is neither essential nor dirty. In casting the one dissenting vote, board member Steve Salisian said that homeowners have jobs that are going begging but the students won't take them . . . "I don't want federal funds taking jobs away from the community."[13]

The Pasadena City Board of Directors entered into a $300,000 NYC contract to provide job opportunities for the poor as file clerks, service station attendants, nursing assistants, golf course trainees, radio shop apprentices, and typist-clerk trainees. After six weeks of extensive publicity in the poverty area (listed as one of the 13 worst poverty areas in Los Angeles County) not one application had been received! A local editorial good humoredly asked, "Where are the Poor?" The editor said:

"What's the next step? Does the city have to surrender federal funds which have been ear-marked for the poor families who either don't exist or don't want them? Or should more funds be appropriated to hire other experts to go out and seek somebody who's poor enough to accept the first funds?

"It's a real dilemma—a surprising turn in fighting a war in which no enemy shows itself." [14]

Strangely enough, the editor, who may have thought he was being sarcastic, came very close to the raw truth. The poverty program *does* pay people to go out and find the poor. It *does* pay someone else to motivate these now-found poor. It *does* pay someone else to train them to be trainable. And it *does* pay someone to coordinate the whole mess. Then on top of all that the community is asked to create a non-essential job in which these poor can learn to work. Naturally, there is also a paid over-all director who supervises the coordinator, the bureau of missing poor, and the psychological impresarios.

However, the most serious complaint comes in the form of potential hanky-panky and straightline patronage. It is quite obvious that many of the non-profit organizations applying for anti-poverty grants are in reality political organizations. Yet under the threadbare cover of "non-profit" or "public welfare," they can request NYC applicants (whose wages are paid for by the federal government) to help in their political programs.

For example, in Los Angeles, Councilman Billy Mills, himself a Negro, complained that the United Civil Rights Committee (UCRC) had no right to have NYC young people working for it.[15] He charged that the group had turned into a political organization . . . but in reality he was worried about UCRC using these tax paid youngsters in their recall campaign against him!

But if Billy Mills is bitter about his tax money going to help finance a recall campaign against himself, how do you feel about helping to finance the Free Speech insurrectionists at the University of California?

Nationally the college end of the Neighborhood Youth Corps program (properly called "Work-Study") was having such a hard time getting enrollees that in 1965 Congress changed the elegibility requirements to be more "flexible." Now college students whose parents earn less than *$10,000* are acceptable and hourly pay scales have been increased to a maximum of $3.00 per hour for these "newly created jobs."[16] And so the left wing warriors at the University of California found a way to fill their pockets while they filled the streets demonstrating against the war in Viet Nam, and the exploitation of the poor by the rotten capitalistic system.

For example, one of the "community action" groups using these Work-Study students (at your expense) is the East Oakland Parish,[17] a "cooperating ministry" founded in 1963 and involved in activities ranging from the abolition of the House

Committee on Un-American Activities to the "get out of Viet Nam" demonstrations.[18] While stirring up trouble among the impoverished by waving the timeworn leftist banner of "police brutality," they are organizing the poor on a block by block basis. They offer the Harlem-type tools of "rent-strikes," "demonstrations," and "picketing." This "parish" is receiving the help of 21 War on Poverty, carefully picked Work-Study students . . . 10 "program assistants," 10 "block organizers," and 1 "program developer." All of this is costing the taxpayer over $16,000 each semester.[19]

The Greater Richmond Parish is a group which focuses on communicating the revelation that "ghetto" life is largely a by-product of the exploitation of the Negro by our capitalistic system. This group has four Work-Study aides (at your expense),[20] and by way of comment they are operating in one of the most explosive Watts-type districts in the Bay area.

The Meiklejohn Civil Liberties Library which is in the backyard of Ann Ginger Fagan Wood (wife of Communist Member James Wood) and which is devoted to civil liberty cases presumably of "dissenters" who have run afoul of the government,[21] has been assigned five Work-Study students at $2.60 and $2.40 an hour.[22]

If there is any doubt in your mind that these Work-Study students are not *carefully picked* to assist these organizations, consider carefully that the Work-Study program at the University is headed by faculty member Joseph D. Lohman who is an open sympathizer of the Student Non-Violent Coordinating Committee.[23]

Coming back to our in-high-school and out-of-high-school Neighborhood Youth Corps, 1965 proved a year of discovering wide-scale violation of the law's supposed intent by the employment of ineligible youths, that is those from non-poor families.

In Kansas City, Kansas, an investigation has shown that more than half of those employed in the NYC program were not eligible for such employment. Participants included one University of Kansas youth who drives to school in a 1965 luxury sports car.[24]

In Jamestown, Rhode Island, Neighborhood Youth Corps organizers admit no effort was made to hire youngsters on the basis of need. Wealthy youngsters were employed to give *sailing lessons* to equally well-off participants in the summer project.[25]

In December, 1965, Los Angeles poverty officials, upset that Washington was insisting on a $3,000 family income limit for NYC youths, stated that up to 70% of those presently employed would be excluded. "It's a serious question," said one EYOA source, "as to whether we could *find* 13,000 youths for the program who would meet the federal criteria."[26] Pasadena's anti-poverty agency (a sort of branch office of the Los Angeles agency) was even more upset at what they called this "unrealistic" and "arbitrary" standard of poverty.[27] Feeling as though they had been bit by the hand that feeds them, they're valiantly fighting to preserve a "high standard" of poverty.

The United States Post Office walked right into a working arrangement between politics and poverty that turned the complexion of the executive mansion from white to a rosy hue.

It seems that nearly half of 8,600 jobs were distributed by the Post Office Department as Congressional patronage instead of going to the high school drop-outs and to the sons and daughters of the poverty-stricken.[28] Evidently, they got lost in the rush of influential Democrats to get their relatives on the Post Office's summer payroll. Many young people from prosperous families held down these $2.29 an hour jobs including the son of a millionaire senator as well as the offspring of many Democrat Congressmen.[29] In Riverside, California, 12 of the 13 jobs went to young people who had actively campaigned for Representative John V. Tunney, 12 of the 13 were Democrats, and few needed the funds for school.[30]

In a hot tempered House debate, the Republicans, led by Congressman Albert Quie, initially put through a resolution which would have forced the Post Office Department to make public the list of summer employees. The original resolution was later defeated when three Democrats (persuaded by White House aides?) changed their votes.[31]

And so, despite the fact that the Post Office might not be considered a part of the federal Economic Opportunity Act as such, one fact stands out: Despite all of its publicly expressed concern for the poor and the unemployed, politicians in the Johnson administration are playing fantastic politics with federal patronage.

All of which brings up the question: Who checks to see that all the jobs and benefits the taxpayer supposedly provides to the poor and the needy really go to the poor and the needy?

So far, the watch-dog role has been assigned to those who benefit politically the most by spending the most. It's quite a show.

Chapter Eleven

NUMERICAL JUNGLELAND

BUREAUCRATS live in a most amazing and wonderful numerical jungleland. It's a necessary climate for they have an infinite ability for spending money and no responsibility for producing it.

All taxpayers are not complete idiots, so the easiest way for the bureaucrat to keep from starving is to play the old number, number, who has the number game. Razzle–dazzle . . . the poor taxpayer is outclassed, out maneuvered, and out spent by the very monster he feeds.

In our efforts to be as statistically accurate as possible we ran into such a dead ripe ripe berry patch of numbers, that at times, pricked to the point of contempt, the easiest thing would have been to sit down and eat the lush berries with the gluttonous bureaucrats.

For example, we were searching for the total enrollment in the Job Corps as of June, 1965. President Johnson announced on May 1 there were 250,000 enrolled,[1] the Office of Economic Opportunity listed on July 21 that there were 9,707 enrolled,[2] and on just one day in July the Congressional Record tally ranged from 10,000 to 304,000.[3]

Neighborhood Youth Corps enrollment was officially announced by the Office of Economic Opportunity to be 265,000 as of June 30, 1965,[4] yet a few weeks prior Sargent Shriver was publicizing the induction of the 100,000th enrollee in a ceremony at the White House.[5]

The records of VISTA volunteers were thrown into the same dealer's shuffle as in most of the other poverty games. On May 15, 1965, Jack T. Conway, then Deputy Director of the Office of Economic Opportunity, publicly stated there were 2,000 VISTA volunteers "going from state to state."[6] Two days later Sargent Shriver announced there were 176 VISTA volunteers.[7] Congressmen's figures (within two days in the Congressional Record) gave us a mid-year leeway of from 136 to 15,000.[8]

You pays your money and you takes your choice! Congressman Odin Langen put it this way:

"It is apparent that the bureaucratic entanglements of the complex Economic Opportunity Act programs have produced a confusing unclear mass of 'approximatelys' and 'expected to be's.' We have not been given the facts, we do not know all the truths."[9]

It is for sure that we are not being given all the facts. How about the Office of Economic Opportunity listing two million more poor farm families than there are total number of farms in the United States as listed by the Department of Agriculture?[10] Maybe these phantom farmers will be given 40 acres and a mule in order to qualify for federal assistance?

Republican Congressmen waited months for the Office of Economic Opportunity to answer the simplest of letters. Congressman Albert Quie requested information on May 28, sent a reminder of the request on June 18, and as the House debated the matter on July 20, was still waiting for an answer.[11] Congressman John Dowdy complained about "the virtual impossibility of getting any information from the sub-princes who control the various sub-programs" at the OEO:

"When the inquiry is by telephone, the person desired is either out of the building, or is on another telephone. The nice secretary who gives the information sweetly promises to have the call returned at once. The call is not returned, and after several such attempts, and some days have passed, one finally loses patience and demands attention, but then receives only inconclusive and unsatisfactory answers to the questions posed.

"With the scores of high salaried bureaucrats and their hundreds of expensive consultants and advisers . . . it does seem that better service could be rendered to Members of Congress who are trying to get information for their constituents."[12]

The press too, has had its troubles—at least those of the press left who are curious enough to try to find out what kind of pill might be underneath the sugar coating. Evidently one such reporter, Mary Packenham of the Chicago Tribune, discovered just how tight bureaucratic controls can be when she was sent to cover a national press conference at the Women's Job Corps Center in St. Petersburg, Florida.

Congressman Charles Gubser told the House[13] that on May 14, Miss Norma Gordon, who was to handle the press conference, called an employee of the Florida Job Corps center from Washington and ordered her to keep Mrs. Packenham under surveillance. The explanation given was that Mrs. Packenham's paper, the Chicago Tribune, was known to be anti-administration and known to be unsympathetic to the Job Corps. Miss Gordon instructed this employee in St. Petersburg to see to it that Mrs. Packenham did not obtain any unfavorable information that she could publish.

We too ran into blank walls in every attempt we made to get honest information. If we had been smart, before attempting to look into the financial aspects of this program, we would have spent a few days at Disneyland riding the merry-go-round in order to acclimate ourselves to the polite but effective run-a-round we were soon to encounter.

Under the name of TAXACTION, Inc., we wrote the Los Angeles City School Department requesting just three things for study by this taxpayers' organization which represents some 75 communities in Los Angeles County: The names of the schools participating in antipoverty programs (poverty areas), the number of anti-poverty teachers employed in these schools (and their salaries), and the number of students enrolled in each of these classes. The request was clarified and limited to just the Watts area in a later phone call, which was then followed by a written reply:

"It would be virtually impossible for our limited staff to compile and complete a report of this scope. Information to complete this report would involve the Elementary Division, Secondary Division, Adult Education section, Work Experience Office, Office of Urban Affairs, and many other operational divisions within the School District."[14]

So, despite one of the most horrifying of insurrections two months prior to this request, despite the riots being blamed in part on lack of education and anti-poverty programs, despite this school district having spent over $4.5 million in eight months on War on Poverty programs,[15] and despite this school district supporting an Office of Urban Affairs whose major job is to oversee and evaluate the city school's anti-poverty programs . . . despite all of these things, it appeared impossible for the Los Angeles City School system to report to a large group of taxpayers what it had done with all of this money in just the one area of Watts.

But by far our most frustrating experience has been our unsuccessful attempt to locate a half million dollars in unaccounted-for funds tangled in the complicated expenditures of the Los Angeles anti-poverty agency, the Economic and Youth Opportunities Agency (EYOA).

A full investigation into the War on Poverty in Los Angeles was ordered by the County Board of Supervisors late in the spring of 1965. TAXACTION had charged duplication of existing programs and political hanky-panky. Supervisors had charged excessive salaries and lack of accomplishment.[16]

The full report was submitted by the Chief Administrating Officer to the Supervisors on July 8.[17] This "full investigation" was nothing more

than a surface report obtained directly from the
agency under investigation! It contained nothing
on salaries, no probings into how the funds were
being administered or how they were checked and
accounted for, and absolutely no evaluation as to
the need for or duplication of some of these poverty
programs.

But the crowning climax to this "full investigation" (which was accepted without question by
the supervisors) was the *obvious unaccounting of
over half a million dollars*. If the supervisors ever
bothered to read the report they requested, they
obviously did not bother to add up the figures.
TAXACTION did.

Representing TAXACTION, Harry Larson, a
CPA and Audit Manager of an internationally
known public accounting firm, went with us to
the EYOA for answers. Leaving out the many
phone calls, delays, and cancellations, a sketchy
resume would go something like this:

"About this half million that doesn't appear to be accounted for—can you explain it
to us?"

"Why certainly . . . that is for our administration of the programs."

"But we thought you received administration costs from other funding sources. Is this
half million for six months in addition to
that?"

"Well now, I guess I was mistaken about
that . . . (call for someone else) . . . oh yes,
this list of figures given to the County Supervisors was not complete and that is why the
figures do not total correctly. There are
funded programs that were overlooked in
compiling this list. And then too, the actual

amounts of funding were not the exact amounts listed."

"May we see a complete and accurate list? Since these fifty some programs are now completed as far as the funding time of the grant is concerned, there must be a financial resume of some sort."

"You realize, of course, the complexity of funding procedures makes a resume like that a most difficult job. We are so short staffed that I am not sure if it has been completed, but I will look into the matter for you and if you will come back ..."

Two weeks later:

"About the up-to-date list of completed programs and the amount of money spent on them?"

"Oh yes, of course. You see many of these programs had money left over and they have been extended on that basis. As a result there has been no final accounting as yet. However, before a new grant is given to them they will be carefully reviewed and evaluated."

"Did these programs have to submit a financial statement to you showing exactly how much money was spent and how much money was left over enabling them to be extended?"

"Oh yes, of course,"

"May we see such a statement, say for just any one or two programs?"

"Certainly. Such reports would be up in our audit department. If you will call for an appointment, I'm sure they will show you whatever you wish."

Days later in the audit department:

"Oh yes, such financial statements are required not just at the close of the grant period, but monthly throughout the course of the programs. We also require each organization to submit monthly evaluations also."

"Wonderful! May we see just one or two?"

"Why of course, but you see we are in the middle of an audit and the auditing firm has all of our records. If you will come back in about two weeks, I am sure we can accommodate you."

Two weeks later:

"I'm so sorry but the audit is running a little over time. Perhaps in another ten days?"

"Is this audit firm auditing just EYOA's books, or are they auditing the financial statements of these organizations which, as subcontracting agencies, have received money from you . . . that is, are they checking to see that so much actually did go for X number of salaries, and so much actually was spent for, say, telephoning?"

"Oh no, the audit is just to verify that we gave X number of dollars under the terms of our contract to each organization administering an anti-poverty program, and that our agency's books balance."

"Then how do you know these organizations actually have used the money for what they said they would?"

"Each organization must submit its own audit to us."

"May we see one or two of these audits?"

"Well, actually none of the organizations has submitted their audits to us as yet . . . the on-going aspect of the program, you know."

"No, I'm not sure we do, but let's go on. We are particularly interested in seeing a list of the paid personnel of two particular programs since we have heard complaints of duplication of personnel. Do you have such a list?"

"For each program?"

"Yes."

"We couldn't possibly require anything like that."

"Surely, someone checks on the list of people these organizations hire with tax money?"

"Not in this department."

"In any department of the EYOA?"

"Not to my knowledge. We can't do everything. That would be a full time job and we are short staffed as it is."

(The EYOA staff salaries run just about $1 million a year!)*

"Then the EYOA has absolutely no way of knowing if the community organizations receiving these federal grants through EYOA are employing known agitators, political leaders, or even active communists?"

"Well, actually no. But of course that is not happening. We can always request the organization to submit us a list of their personnel if we feel it is necessary."

"How soon do you expect the EYOA audit to be completed now?"

"In about ten days. Why don't you come back then and I'm sure we can help you."

Two weeks later:

*See footnote on page 64.

"We're so sorry, the period of the audit was extended so it is taking a little longer than expected."

"Let's forget the audit for the moment. May we see the evaluations of two specific programs which supposedly were completed last June? It is now December and these programs have received a new grant and since we were told that no program, especially these, would be funded again without a complete evaluation, this does seem like a fair request."

(Call for another person.)

"I believe the audit firm has all of those records . . ."

(Raised eyebrows on our part.)
(Call for the new CPA in their audit department.)

"I will be very honest with you. We have had many changes in staff and we have been so rushed with these programs that there has not been an efficient and logical method for either program or fiscal evaluation. We have now set up a new system and intend to proceed on a far more sound basis."

And so it is obvious that large sums of tax money were simply handed over to organizations for the administration of various and sometimes highly experimental programs—some so experimental that they even experimented with eliminating legitimate book-keeping procedures. Then second grants were approved for continuing the same programs without even a comprehensive check as to what had been accomplished, who was employed, or how the money was actually being spent. If any evaluation was done it appears to have been done by the people most involved, which is like hiring the accused to investigate the crime.

And so the story of our meetings with the EYOA continues into 1966. To date we still have no answers to our questions. We are impressed with the polite and cooperative attitude of the EYOA staff, but beyond that we believe that the agency survives in confusions, contradictions, and complete bewilderment. To date, we have yet to see a financial statement or any adequate evaluation. To our knowledge there has been no detailed accounting for the $15 million spent in the first six months of the War on Poverty in Los Angeles and by now there is little likelihood that there ever will be. EYOA has admitted that some funds earmarked for a particular program have been spent on other programs, but beyond that we haven't much to show for over five months of patient waiting and probing.

The EYOA is not the only anti-poverty agency having accounting problems. New York's HARYOU-ACT and Boston's Action-for-Boston-Community-Development (ABCD), to name just two, have both been in serious trouble trying to explain their book-keeping systems.[18]

Our Los Angeles story appears to be alarmingly similar to the Boston fraud scandal that broke in mid-November. A federal investigator said of the Boston anti-poverty agency, "We have found sloppy procedures . . . a lack of top level co-ordination, and disputes among key personnel."[19] He also found *illegal* procedures and an outright *theft* of money, which he failed to mention in his press interview.

There is a difference, however, between Los Angeles and Boston and other cities where irregular, if not illegal, activities are discovered. Boston, at least, had a newspaper, The Boston

Traveler, that was willing to risk investigating, digging into, and exposing the chaotic and illegal activities of their anti-poverty agency; and they substantiated their charges that "fraud, theft, sloppy administration and the political pork barrel have poisoned the $1.8 million project."[20]

Los Angeles, however, continues to be lulled asleep by the Pollyanna approach of the Los Angeles Times, along with most of the major television stations. Not wishing to offend the Great Society, they put both hands over their eyes, and without taking even a little peek, say, "We don't see anything to get so excited about."

There were times early in the fall, when TAXACTION thought about requesting a court order demanding an accounting, and possibly a mistake was made in giving EYOA a chance to clarify the situation . . . to correct the books. "The worst run poverty program in the U.S."[21] will probably turn out to be whitewashed here, as it eventually was in Boston, as a "mistake in book-keeping procedures."

Why does the Los Angeles Times seem unwilling to cast even a local shadow on President Johnson's poverty war? Doesn't it seem strange that while all the stories of scandal and fraud within the program were breaking left and right across the nation, this most powerful paper on the West Coast, chose to print little or absolutely nothing about it all?

Even after Adam Clayton Powell's investigating task force admitted in December that it had received "evidence of mismanagement and fiscal dishonesty"[22] in the Los Angeles anti-poverty program, we still couldn't get the news media to tackle the subject. What we wouldn't have given for an old fashioned, snooping reporter with a "nose" for the news.

The story was—still is—there. The reporter is still missing.*

The bickering, the dissension, the knock-down-drag-out fight, were—still are—part of the story of this War on Poverty. The multi-billion-dollar tax-bone has been thrown out in an open field and, guided by Great Society values, the fight is on.

But . . . there's a new breed of newsmen. The blow by blow call of the fight is, for the most part, being reported through rose colored glasses.

And . . . there's a new breed of anti-poverty warriors in Washington who, as the rather liberal Reporter magazine puts it, are likely to shrug and observe, "War is hell."

"Full steam ahead, they say, throw out the old ways and bring in the new, and let them iron out the local arguments on Main Street." [23]

The local argument was ironed out in Los Angeles on Central Avenue in Watts. To the victor went over $100 million in spoils.

*We found one of the Los Angeles reporters, Paul Weeks, who has long enjoyed executive-like power in his one-sided, happy-Charlie coverage of the War on Poverty for the Los Angeles Times . . we found him last month employed by the Office of Economic Opportunity (Washington) as a full time "Inspector" of the Los Angeles anti-poverty program!

WATTS

Chapter Twelve

WHO POURED THE KEROSENE?

"Los Angeles was a powder keg waiting to have a match put to it." At least so say the professors of human relations in their psychoanalysis of the Los Angeles "Burn, Baby, Burn" riots of August, 1965 . . . the riots which put the small Negro community of Watts in the national spotlight.

Were these riots really ignited by the arrest of a drunken driver? Or were the rioters of Watts truly "rebels with a cause" as was professed? If so, what was their cause, who poured kerosene on their discontent, and did a now forgotten Congressional hearing on the War on Poverty light the match?

Anti-poverty forces played one of the key roles in the intricate pattern which set the stage for this devastating insurrection, and these forces and their allies have been in the limelight of the riot aftermath ever since. Although we have attempted to review the War on Poverty across the nation, we think a close look at the war's activities in Los Angeles before, during, and after the great battle of Watts is in order. These activities form a pattern, and the same pattern can be found in every major city in our nation.

Los Angeles started the War on Poverty with a loud bang. Programs were funded in every direction as quickly as they could be thought up. The Youth Opportunities Board (YOB), made up of representatives from city and county government and schools, proclaimed themselves the official anti-poverty agency. Prior to the August riots in Watts, over 50 programs totaling over $12 million were in operation in poverty areas, and 50 more costing close to an additional $19 million were approved and awaiting funding.[1]

Thus for more than nine months 13 poverty pockets and dozens of organizations had been receiving the benefits (?) of millions of anti-poverty dollars . . . the lion's share having gone to the Watts area. Nevertheless, during that summer, loud and inciting claims were publicized that *"nothing was being done."* Maybe nothing was being done, but plenty was being spent.

From the very beginning, pressure groups had begun to form, demanding that the board of the YOB be expanded to include representatives from the poverty areas.

The YOB readily agreed to appoint such representatives. The Economic Opportunity Act clearly states that there must be "maximum feasible participation" of the poor in these agencies, and to our knowledge no one has ever denied the advantages, even the common sense necessity, of such representation.

But allowing the YOB to "appoint" this representation was completely unsatisfactory to the vocal leaders of the poor. The poor must choose their own representatives through special elections to be held in the poverty areas.

While this demand and its cost were being thrashed out, they brought in their next one. The poor must also have *voting control* of the board.

Nothing could ever really be gained by the poor if they were on a board in which the menacing city hall "power structure" could constantly outvote them. There was constant pitting of the poor against duly elected representatives of the city.

This last demand brought the conflict to a head. *Representation was one thing . . . control was another.*

A few elected officials agreed with TAXAC-TION's stand that, after all, this was taxpayers' money and elected representatives of all the taxpayers should control the spending of it. The Los Angeles Herald Examiner solidly backed this basic concept.[2] There were a few people who felt that if a person was incapable of earning $3,000 a year, he was hardly capable of overseeing a program involving millions. Privately it was whispered that these politically unsophisticated "poor" would be easy targets for the political opportunists . . . a point not to be lightly dismissed.

And so, although efforts to jockey for position had been present from the beginning, it was not until early in the summer of 1965 that the fight began in earnest.

Developments pinpointed the behind-the-scenes Democrat power struggle going on between Governor Edmund Brown and Los Angeles Mayor Samuel Yorty. Governor Brown had apparently given the green light for Joseph Wyatt, long active in the liberal wing of the Democrat party, to organize an anti-poverty agency in opposition to the city-county controlled YOB. Wyatt's new Economic Opportunities Federation sparkled with poverty, labor unions, and ministers.

Mayor Sam Yorty, sneezing with Sacramento fever, could not afford to line up with the Brown forces since gubernatorial primaries were just around the corner.

Sides were chosen, positions taken, and the real war, which is merely *called* the War on Poverty, began.

Civil rights groups began staging meetings in the poverty areas to "discuss" the oppression of the poor by City Hall. Congressman James Roosevelt, still smoldering from the decisive defeat he suffered from Sam Yorty in the Los Angeles mayoralty race a few months earlier, fanned his bitterness into flames of name-calling and revolution-promoting. Loudly backing him were the so-far-to-the-left-binoculars-are-needed-to-find-them Congressman Augustus F. Hawkins, George E. Brown, Jr., and Edward Roybal. These men were supported by a host of others—ministers, union leaders, party men—long associated with militant civil rights movements and socialistic programs. The banner they waved was the right of the poor to run and control their own poverty program.

The persuasive and effective Negro speaker, Rev. H. H. Brookins, put it this way:

"We are not turning back. We are going to send a delegation to Washington . . . this shall be a program by and from the people and not those elected for political reasons."[3]

Discontent among the poor was stirred up by these groups to the point where demonstrations and picket lines were a weekly occurrence during July. Victims of poverty were produced at city council and county board meetings where, in front of television cameras and under the tutelage of men such as Rev. Brookins, they'd parrot the words and attitudes they'd heard preached to them so often.

These people had listened to their local and national leaders. They had heard Martin Luther

King tell them, ". . . we've got to get our freedom, and we've got to get it now."[4]

They had listened to NAACP's Roy Wilkins say, "The Negro has come to the point where he is not afraid of violence. He no longer shrinks back. He will assert himself and if violence comes, so be it."[5]

Congressman Adam Clayton Powell had told them, "Anything we get we will have to fight for, to seize for ourselves. We will invade the white man's heaven, the United States."[6]

Activist William J. Williams, field deputy for Congressman Hawkins, loudly proclaimed that in this fight for the victims of poverty to control the anti-poverty board "we will go to jail if necessary."[7] Under present day criteria, such a stint in jail would no doubt merely enhance Williams' political ambitions . . . he is a Democrat candidate for California's Secretary of State.[8]

Mayor Yorty, obviously busy building his own political machine toward a show-down primary fight with Governor Brown, charged that these activities were a "reckless effort to incite the poor for political reasons."[9] He accused Williams of organizing and leading the demonstrations by the poor both at his city hall office and at his home.[10]

Even the Los Angeles Times said in a July 13 editorial, "Demonstrations have begun, sponsored in part by those who would apparently rather lose the anti-poverty funds if they can't win control of the program." The reference was, of course, to the Augustus Hawkins crowd.

Along about this time in the headline-making battle, it was announced that a Congressional task force from the Education and Labor Committee (headed by Adam Clayton Powell) would come to Los Angeles to "investigate" the uproar and to hold a day of public hearings in the poverty areas. The Congressional members of this all-expenses-paid investigating committee were carefully chosen. It was composed entirely (with the exception of one lone Republican, Alphonzo Bell) of militantly liberal Democrats, headed by (who else?) Augustus Hawkins!

With Hawkins were his Great Society buddies, James Roosevelt (representing the plush Beverly Hills-Wilshire area of Los Angeles County), and Edward R. Roybal (whose district includes much of the Mexican-American community of Los Angeles). All three of these men were firmly in favor of the poor having voting control of the anti-poverty board and bitterly opposed to any compromise plan.[11] Going along for the ride were Congresswoman Patsy Mink and Carlton R. Sickles.

To announce the August 7 Congressional hearing, Congressman Hawkins sent a telegram to the Rev. H. H. Brookins, who frequently carries the ball for him in Los Angeles. Brookins, rather recently transplanted here from Kansas City, seems to have rapidly seized a leadership role. He serves as chairman of the United Civil Rights Committee which is an amalgamation of several dozen militantly aggressive organizations, including a few from the far, far left. He was also chairman of the Hawkins-oriented Community Anti-Poverty Committee which made its bid for control of the anti-poverty structure against the Yorty forces.[12]

Brookins announced the forthcoming Congressional hearing at a press conference at which he was flanked by members of the NAACP, CORE, and other civil rights groups.[13] He said that this hearing would create the "necessary climate in which the poor could express their will . . . we can no longer be treated like children."[14] He went on to say that if the compromise plan (a truce agreement by the Brown-Yorty forces) was approved, the civil rights groups "will take to the streets."

Meanwhile, Congressman Hawkins' own brother, Edward A. Hawkins, a Los Angeles Public Works Commissioner, got into the act by charging his brother with being "investigator, judge and jury." He made this charge in a telegram to Congressman Hawkins which went on to say:

"Neither you nor any members of your committee can possibly preside impartially over a subject matter of which you are personally or partially interested in the outcome."[15]

We attended the "full scale hearing," which was an all-day affair. The session opened in the All Nations Center in the Mexican-American poverty area of Boyle Heights before a standing room audience of more than 500. Typical heated charges and countercharges set the stage for the drama of the hearings.

In the afternoon the scene, but not the script, shifted to the heart of Watts, where a larger audience filled every seat as well as all standing room.

A tape recording was made of the entire proceedings, but no tape could possibly convey to you the atmosphere that was created . . . the tone that was generated by the manner in which information was presented and questions were asked.

We ourselves were almost mesmerized by the revival-like rhythm created by over 1,000 Negroes, swaying and nodding their agreement with the speakers.

At first it was mildly amusing to watch the political jabs Hawkins and Roosevelt were taking at their fellow Democrat, Mayor Yorty (who refused to be present). Then it became disgusting. It is, and always will be, shocking to see duly elected Congressmen behave in such a manner while supposedly conducting a "hearing" for the Congress of the United States of America.

No doubt encouraged by the mass turnouts at both hearings, as well as by the militant position of these poor, Hawkins deliberately aligned himself with those who demonstrate and march in support of their demands. At one point he said, "I will not only participate in a march to City Hall, but will personally lead it myself."[16]

This agitation of public unrest and political party infighting was obvious to us. We knew what they apparently were doing, and probably why. But we doubt if many of the one thousand Negroes sitting in that audience actually understood the political chicanery behind the drama. They were tremendously impressed by the mere presence of live, honest-to-goodness United States Congressmen. They strained just to get a glimpse. They took every word spoken as gospel. They did not see the behind-the-scenes politics.

They heard only phrases that said, in substance: "You are being used. You must organize (with us) and *fight* for your rights. You must not let 'them' continue to take advantage of you. Federal funds are not being administered in a democratic fashion. *Stand up and be heard.* Don't let 'them' continue to ignore you. Demand what is legally and rightfully yours."

Congressman Roosevelt, in expressing his belief that the time for negotiating and talking was over said, "We have negotiated and negotiated until hell has frozen over."[17]

Both Roosevelt and Hawkins had a habit of asking questions of the crowd at large and receiving mass rhythmic answers of "nooo" or "yess," accompanied with cheers, applause, or stamping of the feet.

We were in the back of the auditorium and overheard scattered comments such as: "They're not going to get away with this! Who does Yorty think he is, anyway? We'll show the (censored) we can run this program better than those city hall (censored)."

The air was hot and tense and the "hearing" was nothing more than a political rally. There was no attempt to explain both sides, no attempt to listen to both sides. With a crowd worked up like that, it would have been just plain foolish to attempt another point of view. There was only one correct side and any deviation, no matter how small, was unacceptable.

And yet, while all of this was going on inside the Will Rogers Auditorium, outside hundreds of apparently happy children played contentedly in one of the largest, most beautifully maintained and equipped park playgrounds we've ever seen . . . it even has one of the largest swimming pools in Los Angeles complete with a heated deck (and a total cost of $529,000).[18]

A few blocks away is a beautiful new High School, two other complete park-playgrounds (one has a new $100,000 club house), and two brand new (1960) libraries.[19]

We saw nothing resembling "tenements" or "slums," much less "hunger."*

Four days later this exact area—103rd and Central—was ablaze with fire and hatred, the center

*From the McCone Commission Report (pg. 3): "Watts . . . is a community consisting mostly of one and two-story houses, a third of which are owned by the occupants. In the riot area, most streets are wide and usually quite clean; there are trees, parks and playgrounds. A Negro in Los Angeles has long been

of one of the bloodiest, ugliest examples of wanton human destruction imaginable.

WHY?

One West Coast Congressman, who asked not to be named, was quoted as saying:

"[I have] little doubt but that the hearing is what triggered the riots in Watts . . . giving those people the idea that they were being mistreated was the spark that set off the blast."[20]

able to sit where he wants in a bus or a movie house, to shop where he wishes, to vote, and to use public facilities without discrimination. The opportunity to succeed is probably unequaled in any other major American city."

WATTS

Chapter Thirteen

WATTS FLAMES

THE RIOTS came . . . turning a monotonous heat wave into a fiery nightmare of insurrection. Insurrection: A rising against governmental or political authority; rebellion; revolt; preventing the execution of law, by force of arms. Headlines screamed:

"BLUDGEONINGS AND MOLOTOV COCKTAILS"

"MOB VIOLENCE TERRORIZES ENTIRE CITY"

"BURN, BABY, BURN"

"GET WHITEY"

The Watts insurrection killed 34. More than 1,000 were injured, and 3,438 were arrested.[1] Over $40 million went up in the flames of commercial property damage, not to mention the millions gone up in flames that had been spent on preventing just such a holocaust.

This insurrection necessitated the calling in of 13,900 National Guardsmen in addition to 1,654 local law enforcement officers.[2] This anarchy tore apart the city that less than a year previous the Urban League, a prominent national civil rights organization, had rated *first* among 68 of the nation's largest cities in benefits afforded to the Negro race.[3] These six days cost a fortune in heartache, human relations, unemployment, and tax dollars.

A Negro newsman, here on a visit from Newark, New Jersey, said, "What is going on in Los Angeles makes the Harlem violence look like a quiet Sunday school picnic."[4]

The exhilarating influence of this revolutionary rampage and its army of irresponsible hoodlums spread to Pasadena, where there was looting, sniping, and fire bombs; to Monrovia, Pacoima, Long Beach; and to three days of violence in San Diego, 125 miles to the south.[5]

But in Watts, in Pasadena, in San Diego . . . the quiet backbone of the Negro race, the non-shouting, non-demanding, non-rioting majority, was shocked, horrified, and frightened at what a minority of their race (and ours) was doing to them and to the nation.

But they have been "reduced to silence by the terrorism of the agitational element. Every Negro who has opposed its illegal and senseless actions has been denounced as an 'Uncle Tom,' an enemy of his people and a lackey of the whites . . ." explains George S. Schuyler, the distinguished Negro journalist.[6]

But what excuse do the rest of us have for our cowering submission to the loud-mouthed agitators?

The riots ceased . . . and the aftermath of problems, reports, analysis, and recommendations began. The most touted of all the many groups investigating the uprising was John McCone's "blue ribbon commission" appointed by Governor Brown. McCone, a former chief of the Central Intelligence Agency, had $250,000 tax dollars at his disposal, and 70 staff aides.[7]

One conclusion all of these investigations and reports had in common was *M-O-N-E-Y*. Money had to be spent to correct the ills which caused the riots. If any extensive digging was done into "touchy" areas that might have caused the rioting, such as "communism" or "politics," it was certainly over-looked in the final reports.

It is inconceivable to us that the mass news media and even the esteemed McCone Commission could overlook that fiery, emotion packed, riot-stimulating Congressional hearing of August 7.

It is equally astonishing that the background of Congressman Augustus Hawkins, who represents much of the area where the upheaval took place, could have been overlooked.

Hawkins has been an official sponsor of the Young Communist League,[8] an instructor in two schools sponsored by the Communist Party,[9] and has served on the fund raising committee for the official organ of the Communist Party, the People's World.[10] He has been a member of thirteen organizations cited as Communist Fronts by government bodies.[11] And the Joint Fact-Finding Committee to the Fifty-Seventh California Legislature reported, "Hawkins has consistently followed the Communist Party line."[12]

Of course, when it comes to "following the Communist line" Hawkins is hardly lonesome, as we were to discover in the aftermath of demonstrations, speeches, and recommendations.

While digging into the War on Poverty during these days of riot-itis, we began coming across so many interesting pieces of an unsolved puzzle that we decided to informally compete with Mr. Mc-Cone, once the chief of one of the most influential spy agencies in the world. By doing a little $250,000-less investigating on our own, we discovered, in true "007" ("006" at least) fashion, that lots of innocent questions, lots of listening, and lots of perseverance brought us significant information.

For example, responsible Negro leadership related to us that one night in October of 1964 a group of men representing various militant and hoodlum Negro factions gathered in Los Angeles. Their purpose was to pinpoint on a map principal targets for future vengeance. Primary targets of their destructive fire bombs would be largely Jewish owned business establishments which they felt cheated the Negro buyer with high interest rates and poor merchandise.

The entire plan was by no means confined to just the Watts area of Los Angeles. Indeed, by the time the meeting ended the large, carefully marked map of Los Angeles pinpointed the planned terrorist burning of selected targets over a large area of central Los Angeles.

Ten months later, in the most disastrous riot in United States history, Los Angeles burned. During that destructive rampage not all of the establishments targeted the previous October were put to the torch. Nor were all the buildings that were destroyed part of the original insidious plan. However, too many of the buildings destroyed tallied with the plotted target map to be mere coincidence.

It's possible, of course, that a minor incident, such as interference with officers attempting to arrest a drunken driver, could spark a riot. But is it likely that a full scale rebellion could continue for nearly a week over a three thousand square block battlefield, without the direction of some carefully conceived plan or organization?

Considered this remark picked up by the press: "Hey Yorty, git a fiddle, cause L.A. is burnin'. Didn't we tell ya this was gonna happen?"[13]

The McCone Commission report states they found no evidence of prior planning of the riot. However they did conclude that "the sudden appearance of Molotov cocktails in quantity and the unexplained movement of men in cars through areas of great destruction, support the conclusion that there was organization and planning after the riots commenced" and that "on the tense Thursday, inflammatory handbills suddenly appeared in Watts but could not be identified as a master plan by one group. They rather appear to have been the work of several gangs whose membership of young men range in age from 14 to 35 years."[14]

Police Chief William H. Parker said that the riot started spontaneously but was whipped into greater frenzy by some sort of organization and persons . . . that police radio channels were interrupted by clandestine radio messages during the riot . . . and that the Athens Park* meeting called on the second day of the rioting by John Buggs (director of the Los Angeles County Human Relations Commission) did nothing more than fan the fury.[15]

Billy Graham, while expressing a feeling we all share that an entire race must not be blamed for what a few irresponsible people will do, added that he has reason to believe that "a hard core is

---

*The Athens Park meeting became notorious when major television channels picked up a 16-year-old youth vowing the riot would spread to the white neighborhoods.

at work to destroy our country," and that these race riots are "only a dress rehearsal of what is to come."[16]

Senator George Murphy said that he believed the riots were caused by "a vicious group of trained troublemakers who should be treated for exactly what they are—criminals who have been pampered and pardoned and turned loose time and again by society to create havoc . . ."[17]

Michael Laski, a self-styled member of the Communist Party, said that after the first day party members joined in the "rebellion to attempt to lend form and political expression to the rioters."[18] And the Los Angeles Police, Fire and Civil Defense Committee said in their interim report on the riots that there were "definite patterns" leading to the conclusion that there was some form of organization to the riots.[19]

These conclusions are substantiated by comparing the more favorable conditions for all manner of unrestrained violence in New York City and much of the Eastern United States during the power blackout in December. If wild plundering and arson are truly of a spontaneous origin, then why were there no major disturbances reported in areas of great racial unrest during this ideal period of total darkness? Could it be that aggressive forces were not prepared for the sudden opportunity to foment violence?

Now, we are not going to go off the deep end at this point . . . but piecing together some of our "tidbits" has been a most interesting exercise in self control.

For example, when we find what appears to be a Marxist revolutionist in a key position in the Los Angeles War on Poverty, we just have to react. Ron Ridenour was employed out of the main office of the Los Angeles anti-poverty agency

(EYOA) as a "youth counselor," from February to the end of July, 1965.[20] Ridenour was arrested and deported for distributing Communist literature in Costa Rica following a riot in 1962.[21] Later the State Department revoked his passport when he attempted to enter Cuba.[22] He is an active member of the local DuBois's Club, and co-author of the DuBois's version and interpretation of the Watts riots.[23] He spoke on "An American Radical in South America" at a meeting sponsored by the Young Socialist Alliance" (once with Dan Bessie who is a prominent communist youth organizer) Ridenour[25] was (perhaps still is) a counselor for young Americans in the War on Poverty and his salary for this "counseling" was paid for with your money.

We found it difficult not to react when we learned what happened—rather what *didn't* happen—when Neighborhood Adult Participation (NAPP) employees were checked out by the authorities at the confidential request of Mayor Yorty's office. Out of a list of 400 employees, a large number could not be accurately traced because of lack of proper identification in personnel records (!). But out of those who could be checked, approximately 50 proved to be "poor risks." According to the Mayor's executive assistant, some of these had prior criminal convictions and others were deeply involved in "very far to left" activities. When we asked if these risks would be discharged, we were told such action would not be up to the Mayor . . . "he is just aware that they are there." As we have previously pointed out, "NAPP" employees are in an ideal position to promote political "education" as *they* interpret it!

It bewilders us that the McCone Commission, in their long list of 70 witnesses, could have overlooked a possibly invaluable witness, Jerry Le-Blanc, a Santa Monica Evening Outlook staff writer. LeBlanc spent two months underground, both prior to and including the time of the riots, as a "member of the Extreme Left in Los Angeles." His informative 12 part series appeared in the Outlook beginning September 29, 1965, and should be required reading for the naive or disbelieving.

"Before the fires stopped smouldering, the Extreme Left crews were in action in the riot area trying to help, to blame, and to organize . . .

"John Haag, area DuBois chairman, directed members to channel funds for freeing jailed rioting suspects through the swiftly created "South Side Defense Committee . . .

"The Committee formed to assist riot area Negroes in getting legal assistance, set up headquarters at 326 West 3rd St., the location of the Committee to Protect the Foreign Born, a cited Communist front organization."

LeBlanc told of his experiences as a marcher in the picket lines protesting Police Chief Parker. The marchers were from such far left groups as the DuBois Clubs, Congress of Unrepresented People (COUP) and Committee to End the War in Viet Nam.

According to LeBlanc, two of the most vociferous Marxist revolutionaries said one of the first organizations they called upon to supply pickets for protest demonstrations was the Westminster Neighborhood Association. This is the same organization which, through the "either or else" tactic, received a million dollars of your money to fight their own version of the War on Poverty.

We heard over and over how the Extreme Left formulates the plans for various "peace" or "anti-poverty" demonstrations, then needing manpower to carry them out, they merely notify various churches and organizations of the time and place of the intended demonstration . . . and the members dutifully report!

In reading through issue after issue of The Worker, The People's World, and other Communist publications, we repeatedly ran into articles on the War on Poverty as well as the Watts riots. The theme was always the same: *The War on Poverty is a perfect vehicle through which to promote the Communist beliefs*; nowhere near enough money is being spent on the Poverty War; the Watts riots were not a Communist conspiracy, but a fuse lit by continued acts of police brutality; a citizen's police review board is considered to be essential; and always, they maintain, *control of the poverty program must be in the hands of the poor.*

Now let us make it clear that we are not implying that everyone who advocates these beliefs is a communist. We merely point out that this appears to be the official line of the Communist Party.

The communist method is simple: Bang away, over and over again, that "the people" must "revolt" against "capitalistic oppression." Police brutality is a perfect issue and the organization of the poor under the War on Poverty is the perfect vehicle. The subtle approach is used to reach the more sophisticated, while local magazines, such as The Liberator, pitch with less finesse:

" . . . with bottles, bricks, and bullets they [Watts] tried to repay Chief Parker's racist cops for years of beatings, killings, false arrests, and for the tyrannical, arrogant, storm trooper attitude which the police have towards the Black community."[26]

(Let's take just a moment for a breath of fresh air: Chief William H. Parker is recognized the world over as one of the finest of police authorities, and is the official symbol of law and order in Los Angeles.)

Charges of police brutality and demands for a citizens' police review board came, not only from all of these fancy named lefty groups and openly communist publications, but from the more established "solid" organizations and people of the left as well.

Adam Clayton Powell was quick to insist that the first step in restoration of relations between the races in Los Angeles must be the dismissal of Chief Parker whom he termed "a symbol of racial persecution."[27] CORE, backed by demands for Parker's dismissal from their national director, James Farmer, led sit-down, lie-down, and every-other-kind-of-down demonstrations for the Chief's removal.[28] The "non-political" United Civil Rights Committee (Rev. H. H. Brookins) was in on the demands,[29] as was the American Civil Liberties Union.[30] Los Angeles City Councilman, Billy Mills,[31] State Assemblyman Mervyn Dymally,[32] and Congressman Augustus Hawkins[33] were right in there pitching. The only real shock we had was to discover the Pasadena YWCA sponsoring the Community Relations Conference of Southern California which released a long and no-mistake-about-it critical thesis against Chief Parker.[34]

Martin Luther King came to Los Angeles shortly after the riots, accompanied by Bayard Rustin ("Mister March"), and spoke at the Westminister Neighborhood Association center in Watts. King reminded the people that "for year after year the

Negro has been the victim of terrible brutality by policemen . . . even sheriffs." He advocated the immediate establishment of an independent police review board, and that there is a "very urgent need at this hour" for the federal anti-poverty program to alleviate economic want.[35]

John A. Buggs, executive director of the Los Angeles County Commission on Human Relations (remember what great praise Saul Alinsky had for Buggs), took advantage of his $18,000 a year salary to improve human relations by charging that police intensified the riots by trying to quell it with white policemen and by refusing to take *his* advice and that of other race relations experts. According to an October 22 newspaper account,[36] "Buggs said that he and others were in touch with leaders of the riots August 12 and said they had assured him the riots could be ended then if white policemen were kept out of the riot area and if 'someone would get on the television and say that we [the rioters] are not hoodlums but rebels with a cause.'"

REBELS WITH A CAUSE!

As far as many of the looters were concerned beer, gin, and a new sofa for the living room appeared to be sufficient "cause."

And by way of comment on Mr. Buggs . . . if he knew who the leaders of the riots were on the second day of the nightmare, why weren't the police informed? Or in their clan would that be considered squealing?

In the same vein of "human relations," the Rev. James E. Jones, a member of the Los Angeles city school board and appointed by Governor Brown to serve on the seven man McCone investigating commission, ranted on August 12 that the riot was "mainly the outlet of years of pent-up frustration, harassment and the brutality which has been perpetrated upon Negroes."[37] And in a well publicized dissent with his fellow members on the McCone Commission he wrote: "Protest against forces which reduce individuals to second class citizens, political, cultural, and psychological non-entities, are part of the celebrated American tradition."[38] Surely Rev. Jones is not suggesting that the Watts riots were in a "celebrated American tradition"?

Another prominent Negro leader whom we have mentioned before, Rev. H. H. Brookins, testified to the McCone Commission that had positive steps been taken in time "none of the rioting would have taken place." He claimed that "disinterest by the white power structure" created a climate that led to the eruption.[39]

Church leaders joined the hue and cry. Picking at random one of the many ecclesiastical comments, Methodist Bishop Gerald Kennedy said, "We need to break the logjam on this War on Poverty . . . I think church leaders must yell until they hear us."[40] Yell. Demand. Threaten.

A prominent Negro author and speaker, Louis Lomax, who conducts a popular weekly television show, said that both Parker and Yorty "unbelievably maligned" Negro leadership by charging they were unable to control rioters in Watts.[41] Are we to presume by that, that if it is maligning to say these leaders couldn't control the riots, then these leaders could, in reality, control the situation but simply *chose not to?*

Lomax called on the Negro community to lay bare the issue of police brutality . . . "I want the white community to see five or six thousand women with babies in their arms, telling of beatings in their stomachs," he said. "Such a massive demonstration could not be ignored."[42]

So spoke the Negro leaders . . . in what appeared to be the most feeble effort in history to pour oil on troubled waters.

Los Angeles county Sheriff Peter J. Pitchess, emerging tight-lipped and serious from his testimony to the McCone Commission, said simply to eager newsmen, "Too many people have done too much talking already."[48]

Chapter Fourteen

WHO'S SICK?

WHETHER it be Harlem or Watts, Chicago, Philadelphia or Rochester, the same sick pattern is repeating itself over and over with alarming frequency and similarity. Police brutality charges, demands for civilian review boards, marches on City Hall, militant human relations commissions, demonstrations, picketing and threatening, "incidents" sparking riots. Revolution. Insurrection.

The raucous demands form a pattern which weaves intricately in and out of the War on Poverty. The War on Poverty, because of its political philosophy, has a large place in any explanation of rioting in Watts or Harlem or any other American city . . . not as a solution, but as a factor.

We can poke fun in some places at the War on Poverty. We can ridicule in other places. Sometimes we can have a good old laugh. But here . . . there is no humor.

We watched a large belt of our city go up in useless flames and it was a frightening and horrifying experience. We knew some of the more specific circumstances preceding the outbreak and this was even more frightening. But worst of all is what is now being crammed down our throats in the reports of sociologists, psychologists, and ministers, by militant civil rights groups, and by committees, commissions, and cranks.

The blame for such open disregard of the law is not put on those who threw Molotov cocktails, is not put on those who threw Molotov cocktails, is not put on those who threw rocks and shot at firemen attempting to put out the fires, nor is it put on those who stole and looted, who destroyed and killed, who disobeyed the most basic laws of man, country, and God. The blame isn't even put on those who incited (sometimes intentionally and professionally) this mob violence.

Perhaps a slight smile of unbelief is in order here, because what is being said by a high-titled minority and apathetically accepted by a confused majority is truly stranger than fiction. The blame for all this wanton destruction is being put on the law-abiding citizens who did nothing more violent than to stay home shaking with fear and anger, silently paying the bills of the Great Society. *They* are the ones who cause these bloody, horrifying scenes of insurrection! *They* ". . . built the theater, set the stage, and wrote most of the script leading to the terrible drama in Los Angeles and other recent racial explosions in the nation."[1]

We must understand that these people "feel morally right about what they have done," said Dr. Harold W. Jones, a Negro psychiatrist in charge of a tax supported mental health clinic in the Watts area. "They look upon it as a revolt rather than a riot and therefore subject to a different value system. They see their insurrection as an opportunity to achieve dignity and self-respect. It is as if they are saying, 'It's better to be feared than to be held in contempt.' "[2]

C.T.M. Hadwen, professor of sociology at the University of Southern California, said the rioters were "exhilarated and happy because for once they were released from their customary role of patient, long suffering victims of white indifference."[3]

Two sociology professors expounded that although the Los Angeles riots were deplorable, they "illustrated the fundamental Marxian concept of conflict's importance in a developing social system." Marx's sociological writings are a "magnificent heritage," they added . . . and got headlines in the Los Angeles Times.[4]

We must never forget that "magnificent heritage."

As conscientious professionals, these social-ills doctors are not content to just diagnose. Their prescriptions have remarkable logic in view of their diagnosis: Do more . . . give more . . . spend more.

As a precautionary measure, just in case we think we can afford a guilt complex more than the prescription, we are told that cost can not be considered . . . you can not measure the ills of society in terms of dollars and cents.

How much more "ill" can a nation get when it becomes morally and financially bankrupt?

In a nutshell, we are being told that if we had given more in programs, privileges, and benefits ($) to these rioters they would have been motivated to take advantage of the opportunities already offered them and none of this would have happened. Further, if we don't give more as quickly as possible, to the poor, the depressed, and the unemployed, it will happen again.

Right now we can name half a dozen cities where riots far worse than those of Watts are being systematically predicted (and thus suggested) unless the poverty platter is passed immediately. Oakland! Washington, D.C.! Chicago! Watts, again?

This carefully organized (at your expense) business of "either or else" is the little child's tantrum act in grownup terms. It can be, and evidently is, darned effective!

Senator Robert Kennedy said that it was "pointless to tell Negroes living in northern slums to obey the law . . . the law is the enemy."[5]

The Senator's solution?

" . . . only massive anti-poverty . . . programs can eventually turn the tide away from lawlessness."[6]

He acknowledged that there would be ample stealing and graft in the programs. But, he added, people will just have to live with it and *understand* it.

Chapter Fifteen

THE PASSWORD IS WATTS

"The riots may not be the right way, but it's a way. At least they are listening to us." [1] So said one Negro resident of Watts . . . and how right can you be?

Once the riots quieted down, the break-neck pace in requesting federal funds was strictly of the survival-of-the-biggest variety. Reports of the *federal* anti-poverty money pouring into Watts from September to the end of the year ran something like this:

$1.7 million to be used to hire the poor to clean up riot torn Watts . . . limit of $500 materials per house. [2]

$29 million ordered by President Johnson for rehabilitation of Watts. [3]

$150,000 federal grant for a "sensitivity workshop" for teachers from disadvantaged school areas. [4]

$7.4 million released to EYOA for Community Action poverty programs.[5]

$16.5 million to Los Angeles city schools for poverty programs under the Elementary and Secondary Education Act (later this figure was quoted at $12.1 million).[6]

$300,000 for Community Action programs funded by the bypassing of the Los Angeles anti-poverty agency (EYOA).[7] (There is no way of knowing how much is funded via this route, unless a newspaper digs it up.)

$1 million to the Westminister Neighborhood Association for a job training program.[8]

$417,500 to set up four day care centers accommodating 300 children and 450 employees.[9]

$5 million to Los Angeles City School's poverty programs. The list included funds for pre-school classes, extended day, Saturday school, group counseling, student achievement center, parent-child preschool, guidance, counseling, and testing, home management, reception room program, school opportunity center, parentschool coordination, etc. Most of these programs were being re-funded since they had been in operation for the past year under War on Poverty funding.[10]

$27 million available to Los Angeles schools for poverty programs involving "bold imaginative thinking" according to Wilson Riles, executive secretary of the State Advisory Compensatory Education Commission and benefactor to liberal civil rights philosophers.[11]

$6 million received by EYOA to continue and to expand the "in-school" Neighborhood

Youth Corps (bringing the total to $13.5 million since February).[12]

$1 million to Mexican American neighborhoods for employment and remedial education programs.[13]

$1 million released for Community Action programs through EYOA (bringing total to $30 million since February).[14]

$2.9 million to finance two new manpower centers to provide job training, a family counseling program, and a pre-school program.[15]

$141,890 to rehabilitate youth gangs in the Watts area.[16]

$8.2 million for continuation of the Head Start program.[17]

$400,000 for repair and demolition of unsafe structures in Watts resulting from the riots ($100,000 city money).[18]

$227,542 to educate teachers working in poverty areas.[19]

$273,690 to conduct experimental job shop.[20]

$15 million requested for Governor Brown's program to train 5,000 persons in the riot area. "This is not an expensive program," he said. In explaining about paying these while in training he said, "This money is given to them just like unemployment insurance. It is given to them as part of a social dividend for being citizens of this great country . . . ."[21]

$379,900 for a new "one-stop" employment office in East Los Angeles that will house eleven different government agencies offering services deemed vital to assisting Watts to recover.[22]

$12 million for city to employ and partially educate 2,000 from poverty area.[23]

$8.4 million for city to employ (but not to provide education classes) 1,500 to 2,000 unskilled adults in city clean-up and beautification.[24]

$98,000 for city to draw up plans for rebuilding riot shattered Watts, and *$4.4 million* in grants set aside for area when planning is complete.[25]

$2.25 million for a vocational rehabilitation program similar, we assume, to what we described in chapter five.[26]

$356,288 for an on the job training program to serve 600 unemployed from Watts.[27]

$7 million for the University of Southern California to set up health clinics in Watts (question whether these funds would be contracted through EYOA or directly from Washington).[28]

Not all of this money has been received, but on the other hand this represents hardly a fraction of what is being requested. The McCone Commission recommends programs that make all of this seem like a mere downpayment. The city schools alone estimate that they would need an additional $250 million annually to carry out the McCone plan to educate the poor.[29]

If Los Angeles County discounts the fantastic cost of the riots in damage, in commission inquiries, and in court hearings and processing, it still has over *$400 million* a year spent on routine welfare programs[30] ($5.5 million *monthly* in the riot area alone.)[31] It still has the multi-millions of dollars spent in *existing* school, recreation, and probation department programs. The Department of Employment maintains over 50 Youth Employment Service (YES) centers in this area.[32] United Way collected $19 million in contributions from this county last year.[33] There are retraining programs by government agencies, private industry, and private non-profit foundations. On War on Poverty programs alone, Los Angeles County has spent $41,257,768.[34] Would you be willing to hazard a guess on how much is being offered that we haven't even thought about listing?

And yet the cries persist: "Unless something is done for the Negro community," they say, "there is no telling what holocausts will result."

The password to the tax tills is simply "WATTS." Just ask for it by name.

Attending the Los Angeles anti-poverty board meetings (which by now had settled down to a 23 member board with seven representatives from the poor) became torture. We watched while Archie Hardwick, executive director of the Westminster Neighborhood Association of Watts (the same association referred to before) submitted a 45 page, $1 million, program proposal.[35] Giving the board *no* time to even glance at the contents, he asked for their approval. Some members balked, saying they could not approve something they hadn't even read. But Hardwick, in true trick-or-treat spirit informed them that the "tensions" in Watts were so explosive that if this program wasn't approved immediately, he would be deeply concerned about what might happen . . . and besides, since Washington had already promised the money directly, he was just trying to create good will and better relationships by submitting it to the board in the first place. The program was approved within five minutes of the time it was submitted, and one official later mumbled "political blackmail."

One million dollars worth!

Then there was "supermarket" day at the board.[36] A plan to centralize all the offices of all kinds of welfare agencies in one three or four block area of Watts was described to the board as a sort of "supermarket" of social service agencies. It was said that much of the unrest in Watts is due to the fact that many Negroes do not know of all that is available to them through welfare programs, and others do not have the transportation or inclination to get to the downtown offices (at least four or five miles distant).

It was explained to the board that the "supermarket" would be a place where a woman could go to one office and pick up her Aid-To-Families-With-Dependent-Children check, then go right next door to a child care center where she could leave her children while she went to still another building to receive "prevocational" training or charm-grooming courses. Another building would house the medical check-up offices, and eventually they hoped to have a hospital to take care of her illnesses. Social Security, unemployment, and general welfare offices would be here also. Psychiatric help, child guidance, legal aid, consumer education centers, and anti-poverty offices. We should probably throw in for good measure a Traveler's Aid office . . . after all if Traveler's Aid Society can use our tax money to finance a 24 hour mobile unit to assist poverty migrants on the freeways, it certainly ought to offer help to the poverty-stricken soul attempting to find his way from one office to another in this four or five block agency complex.

The "supermarket" was given the green light[37] with absolutely no one thinking to ask if "S & H Green Stamps" would be part of the bargain.

And so under the War on Poverty we are organizing the poor to teach them how to get more out of existing welfare laws and how to demand more welfare legislation. Then, to make things even easier, we finance a central supermarket of agencies so they won't have to put themselves out to take what they haven't earned. And they shall be slaves to their benefactor . . . the great and generous federal government.

In Altadena there is a parrot named Poverty Pete. He sits in his cage and says, "Gimme . . . gimme . . . gimme."

We sat at EYOA board meetings and listened while plans for the election of the poor were hashed out. If you are not familiar with this idea, let us explain.

This is a new kind of special-privilege election, in which only the poor elect only other poor to an anti-poverty board where they busy themselves spending *our* money. To vote in this uniquely un-American election you do not have to be a citizen, you do not have to register, you do not have to be 21, you do not have to be able to read or write (not even your own name). All that is required is that you be willing to state that you are poverty stricken . . . which in Los Angeles terms is earning (receiving) less than $4,000 a year. Then you vote for someone else who states he does not have an income of more than $4,000 a year (this is important in administering a multi-million dollar program), is at least 21, and, if the EYOA is not mistaken, is a citizen.[38]

The Los Angeles version of this private election to place seven members from the poor on the EYOA board was launched with great bally-hoo-hoo. Fifty five "poor" declared themselves candidates. One such person, Albert L. Roma, described himself as a poor man with eight people besides himself to support. He had been working as a NAPP (Neighborhood Adult Participation, page 70) employee for $4,000 a year, but decided to give up this job in order to run for the non-paying job of representing the poor on the Los Angeles anti-poverty board. While the Pasadena paper seemed overwhelmed with the solemn dedication of this man to his fellow kind,[39] we are overwhelmed about what is going to happen to his wife and seven children now that he has been elected!

As election day approached, newspapers, television, and the radio gave the March 1 event as much publicity as a regular election . . . you know, the kind where you don't have to be poor to vote. Over 600 "volunteers" (the federally paid type of NAPP volunteers?) conducted block to block campaigns in an extensive effort to "get-out-the-vote." Eight sound trucks were used, and over 300,000 pieces of literature were distributed (all at your expense). Polling places (154) were set up in practically every high school throughout the county including such places as wealthy San Marino and Beverly Hills, "so poverty stricken domestic workers could conveniently get to the polls." The polls were open from 7 a.m. to 9 p.m. . . . longer than any "normal" election.[40] You see, in other cities where such elections have been held, the percentage of eligible poor that bothered to vote has been as low as 4%[41] and the EYOA had no intention of flubbing the national importance to the War on Poverty of this election.

Election day came and went. The end result was a sickening and pathetic farce. Of the 400,000 ballots printed, only 2,659 were used. That's just *one half of one percent!* That's barely fifty votes per candidate! That's pretty sickening![42]

Of course the excuses were quick to come. "There hadn't been enough publicity . . . the poor weren't well enough informed about what was going on . . . many poor were reluctant to declare how much or how little their income was . . . we haven't spent enough money 'motivating' and 'educating' the poor . . .", etc. etc. etc. One official from the EYOA explained on television that the first of the month was a terrible day to hold an election . . . most of the poor didn't want to leave home because that was the day their welfare checks arrived.[43] And to our way of thinking . . . that explanation did it!

What is happening to our common sense? Why not have an election in which only the executives of million dollar corporations can vote to determine how our tax money is to be spent? It's far more sensible . . . but hardly democratic.

Elected representatives of *all* the people should control the spending of tax dollars whether it be federal, state, or local tax money. It's just that simple and why get it all colored up in the hazy greys of a cock-eyed philosophy?

In this current tide of social revolution and whirlwind spending, we find all the militant civil rights groups. The United Civil Rights Committee is seeking $250,000 from the Office of Economic Opportunity to conduct a voter education and registration program in Watts.[44] The whole point of this program is simply to build a political machine at taxpayers' expense. As the March 3, 1966, KNX/CBS editorial pointed out, if the 400,000 "poor" people of Los Angeles could be lined up as a bloc, its leaders would just about control politics and public money in Southern California.

Convinced as we have become of the real purpose behind this Great Society program, we still receive rude jolts when we see it spelled out in neon lights. But then, as Columnist George Jordan quips, "People who seem surprised to find politics in the War on Poverty would expect a fighting cock and a bantam hen to produce love birds."[45]

The Office of Economic Opportunity is, undoubtedly, going to continue to play footsy with these extremely militant and vigorously political civil rights leaders. How else would you interpret the resignation of James Farmer as National Director of CORE in order to head up a national anti-poverty "literacy" program? Sargent Shriver is expected to authorize a "setting up" budget of $860,000.[46]

Columnists Evans and Novak on January 13, 1966, pointed out that James Farmer is "an old line Norman Thomas Socialist and pacifist" and not likely to occupy himself wholly with Adult Education in this program. The board of directors of this new War on Poverty venture contains members from every major civil rights organization (from SNICK to the Urban League). Legal counsel for the program is Farmer's more radical successor to head CORE, Floyd McKissick. Evans and Novak refer to McKissick, with his "black nationalism," as the disrupting force at the White House conference on civil rights last fall, calling for dismantling the capitalistic system.[47]

Even official advocates of urban renewal schemes are looking with envy at the easy money afforded to their bureaucratic sister-in-law, the War on Poverty. Rex Vance, field representative of the federal Housing and Home Finance Agency, told Pasadenans in late August that renewal laws were old hat, and that President Johnson's War on Poverty is the new touchstone for renewal. He called the anti-poverty drive "the very cornerstone of urban renewal" and begged Pasadena to take advantage of it:

"Our own kind of urban renewal program is getting kind of old now," Vance said. "It has lots of rules and regulations. But the War on Poverty program is wide open. Use your imagination and ingenuity . . . the OEO have funds which are going begging."[48]

So the Office of Economic Opportunity has funds that are going begging. How's *your* bank account? Senator Everett Dirksen said:

"I will vote nothing for the kind of program that has now been diffused all over America, and that will become probably the greatest boondoggle since bread and circuses in the days of the ancient Roman Empire, when the republic fell. I will be no party to it . . .

"We are on a binge—it cannot last."[49]

And what has the reaction been to this multibillion dollar spending binge?

A Los Angeles city councilman urged an additional $100 million be spent to *"give the Negro people of Los Angeles something to live for."*[50]

The California Negro Leadership Conference asked for *$500 million* for a California Public Works program to relieve Negro unemployment.[51]

Mr. A. Phillip Randolf, honorary chairman of the meeting to plan the White House Civil Rights Conference this spring asked for *$100 BILLION* (that's almost equal to the nation's entire budget) to wipe out Negro ghettos. "THINK BIG" was the advice given to the members. And it was mentioned that the American people were to be made to remember that any cost is cheap compared to the cost of another Watts.[52]

In other words, surrender is cheap compared to the cost of war.

Remember Watts!

Chapter Sixteen

WHO'S ANGRY NOW?

When are we going to get angry? Not irritated . . . ANGRY? Have we completely lost our capacity for outrage?

One Los Angeles teacher got angry. In fact he became so disgusted at what was really going on in this War on Poverty that he prepared what he calls "A Summary Affidavit: An Inside View of the

War on Poverty." It was important enough and effective enough to be entered in the Congressional Record on October 19, 1965, by Congressman H. R. Gross.

The entire report is fascinating, but we will pull out just a few excerpts from Mr. Bruce Shawyer Glenn's account of his experiences at John Muir High School in Los Angeles during the reign of anti-povertyism.

"In midspring 1965, an official of the federal anti-poverty program . . . spoke at a regular faculty meeting of the school." This official urged the teachers to come up with more creative ideas to spend all this War on Poverty money, that applications for funds had been slow, and that "almost anything" would be approved.

This official then said, and we continue to quote Mr. Glenn, that "We Americans were going to have to change our way of thinking a great deal to accept the idea of men never working in their entire lifetimes, but living from cradle to grave on federal welfare. Those of us 'fortunate' enough to have jobs would, through taxes, support those so 'unfortunate' enough to be permanently unemployed."

(We are going to interrupt Mr. Glenn's story long enough to comment that all of this nonsense about one group having to support another group because there won't be enough jobs for everyone is just so much malarky, unless, of course, we allow the kind of people who preach such lunacy to ruin our free enterprise system. Then and only then could such a conclusion be valid. When you say there are not enough jobs to go around, you must add "of the kind I'm willing to accept and at the salary I'm willing to take." As long as it is more profitable to keep rocking instead of working there is going to be unemployment.)

Mr. Glenn was chosen (as being in the top ten percent of the teaching staff) to attend a National Defense Act Institute which was set up as a part of the War on Poverty at California State College in Los Angeles from June 21 to July 30, 1965. Each teacher received "$450, nontaxable, for the six weeks." The purpose of the Institute was to "aid teachers of disadvantaged youth and to give them an inside view of the War on Poverty."

One of the three books listed as required reading for the course was "The Other America" by Michael Harrington, the outspoken foe of the free enterprise system. Suggested reading included books by Howard Fast, long associated with leftist activity, Ann Braden, "an identified Communist whose husband is the longtime organizer for the Communist Party in Kentucky," and two by Herbert Aptheker, "a member of the National Committee of the Communist Party, U.S.A. and its chief theoretician."

As part of the activities of the Institute the teachers visited the headquarters of the Neighborhood Adult Participation Project (NAPP) with its offices, outposts, storefronts, substations, neighborhood assemblies, and blockworkers."

Mr. Glenn comments that all of these sound "too much like the civilian spy networks of Nazi Germany or Soviet Russia" and he adds that he has studied, in depth, the governmental apparatus of these systems at both the undergraduate and graduate levels.

The NAPP director told the visiting teachers that "all traditional channels of welfare" had to be either changed or discarded. A planning director for the south area spoke of "the desirability of 'replacing' most, if not all, existing welfare agencies—both public and private—with 'community-oriented and managed agencies' financed exclusively by the federal government."

During the Institute's meetings a taped speech by Michael Harrington was played after which no discussion was allowed. Mr. Glenn says "Harrington referred sneeringly to the States as 'historical accidents.'" Later at an Institute luncheon "an officer in the department of Urban Affairs of the Los Angeles Schools and one of the official school representatives on the Los Angeles anti-poverty board confided in us that the reason for all the hassle over the distribution of 'poverty funds' all over the United States was that the War on Poverty was the 'deathblow to the States,' which would soon be reduced to 'administrative districts.' He went on to say that State Legislatures and even the State Governors would soon be of little importance."

Mr. Glenn recounts that teaching members of the Institute's staff held seminar discussions during which the enrolled teachers were told that Americans were facing total societal change of the kind outlined by Michael Harrington and the Center for Democratic Studies. It was explained most matter of factly that these proposals would put one-third of the nation on Federal Welfare. A staff member said "that our sovereignty as free individuals must be lessened" and that "freedom of action must be curtailed to aid those on the low end."

Quoting directly from Mr. Glenn's testimony: "We were told . . . how those who oppose this 'total societal change' and who wish to reinforce traditional values should be dealt with. Relying mainly upon works by George D. Spindler, the staff member stated that 'cultural therapy' was needed by 'reaffirmative traditionalists' so that they could adjust to our changing society. A 'reaffirmative traditionalist' is described as being individualistic, practicing strict morality, believing in hard work and stressing the value of education. In detail, 'cultural therapy' is designed to 'strip an individual's defenses; expose him to public view; and get the individual to a state of not knowing whether he is coming or going.' Then reorientation can begin."

Mr. Glenn tells of how he was an observer at a summer opportunity center, financed entirely by the War on Poverty, at Charles Drew Junior High School in the core of the area later to be torn apart by the Watts riots. He states that he was at the school twice a week from July 6 through 29, 1965, and makes the following comments:

"Young female students would attend classes wearing only a halter and very lowcut hipslingers."

"Many of the students—male and female— would arrive at the school drunk. This was at 8:30 in the morning."

"Obscene language, threats, and fights, were the rule not the exception."

He adds the following post script:

"It should be held firmly in mind that all the quotations . . . are from persons who are proponents of the War on Poverty. None of their remarks were intended to be critical of the federal antipoverty program.

"Also, it cannot be emphasized strongly enough that the War on Poverty is a federally

Mr. Glenn ends his testimony by saying that "I hereby attest that this document in every detail and essential is accurate, and I will so swear if called upon to do so, under oath."

enacted program, operating on federal tax moneys, under direct federal control. It is a local program only in the sense that local people may become a part of it. Thus what is related in this affidavit holds true regardless of whether you are speaking about the effect of the program in California or Iowa, Maine or Texas.

"If the United States of America as it was conceived and constituted is to survive the War on Poverty all freedom-loving citizens of whatever race, color or creed must unite in opposition to it."

We reaffirmative traditionalists would rather fight than switch!

A FINAL WORD FROM
THE PUBLISHER

AMERICA will never win a War on Poverty by destroying the individual initiative of her citizens.

Let us not trade our principles for a mass of old worn-out ideas with new and fancy labels. If our system should fail it will be because we developed something more deadly than a hydrogen bomb, and that is a philosophy—an idea which says that the individual is no longer economically responsible for his own welfare or morally responsible for his own conduct.

So let us be done with extravagant expenditures and corrupting influences and with battle plans which humble and degrade, lest we become a nation of beggars crying:

"PASS THE POVERTY PLEASE".

DOCUMENTATION

Chapter 1:

1. Congressional Record: August 18, 1965, p. 20076
2. New York Daily News: February 28, 1966
3. Al Capp: "Little Abner," January 12, 1966
4. New York Times: March 5, 1964 (County Departments of Planning and Public Welfare)
5. U. S. News and World Report: January 17, 1966, p. 14
6. Congressional Record: July 21, 196 , p. 16961
7. Congressional Record: July 20, 1965, p. 16891
8. John Chamberlain: Los Angeles Herald Examiner, October 28, 1965
9. Congressional Record: August 18, 1965, p. 20086
10. Wall Street Journal: April 20, 1965
11. Economic Opportunity Act of 1964: Public Law 88-452

Chapter 2:

1. AP release: Los Angeles Times, May 29, 1965
2. Congressional Record: July 21, 1965, p. 16973; July 22, 1965, p. 17315; and August 14, 1965, p. 19804
3. Congressional Record: July 20, 1965, p. 16889
4. Robert S. Allen & Paul Scott: Human Events, January 1, 1966
5. ibid.
6. Los Angeles Times: May 29, 1965
7. AP release: Los Angeles Times, April 12, 1965
8. Wall Street Journal: May 13, 1965
9. Congressional Record: July 20, 1965, p. 16872
10. AP release: Los Angeles Times, December 15, 1965
11. UPI release: Los Angeles Herald Examiner, December 9, 1965
12. AP release: Los Angeles Times, August 27, 1965
13. George Jordan: "Seasoning the News," The Orange County Republican, January, 1966
14. New York Times magazine: November 22, 1964, p. 39
15. Bruce Shawyer Glenn: Testimony in Congressional Record, October 19, 1965
16. League for Industrial Democracy letterhead: November 30, 1965
    New York Times: November 19, 1964
17. Bruce Shawyer Glenn: Testimony in Congressional Record, October 19, 1965
18. ibid.
19. Alan Stang: *It's Very Simple*, Western Islands, Boston & Los Angeles, 1965, pp. 165-166

20. League for Industrial Democracy: Biographical sketch
21. Human Events: December 11, 1965
22. Congressional Record: July 20, 1965, p. 16852
23. Congressional Record: July 20, 1965, p. 16879-83
24. ibid.
25. Readers Digest: January, 1966
26. Congressional Record: July 21, 1965, p. 16959
27. Carl T. Rowan: Los Angeles Times, January 12, 1966
28. Los Angeles Times: January 12, 1966
29. Ruth Montgomery: Los Angeles Herald Examiner, November 17, 1965
30. Lyndon B. Johnson: White House Speech, January, 1964
31. ibid.
32. The Houston Post, July 10, 1965
33. Wall Street Journal, February 18, 1966
34. Taped speech of Saul Alinsky as given to Los Angeles County Human Relations Commission, July 1, 1965
35. The Reporter: June 3, 1965, pp. 19-22
36. Los Angeles Times: September 8, 1965
37. The Reporter: July 15, 1965, p. 34
38. Congressional Record: July 22, 1965, p. 17281
39. Richard Wilson: Los Angeles Times, September 2, 1965
40. Fulton Lewis Jr.: Los Angeles Herald Examiner, November 2, 1965
41. Congressional Record: July 22, 1965, p. 17286
42. Wall Street Journal, February 18, 1966
43. The Reporter: July 15, 1965, p. 34
44. ibid.
45. Look: July 27, 1965
46. Indianapolis Star: August 5, 1965
47. Taped speech of Saul Alinsky as given to Los Angeles County Human Relations Commission on July 1, 1965
48. Dan Smoot Report, March 14, 1966
49. The Reporter: June 3, 1965, pp. 19-22

Chapter 3:
1. Economic Opportunity Act (Public Law 88-452): Title 11, Part A, Sec. 205 (a)
2. Congressional Record: August 19, 1965, p. 20357
3. Economic Opportunity Act (Public Law 88-452): Title 11, Part A, Sec. 202 (a)
4. Economic Opportunity Act (Public Law 88-452): Title 11, Part A, Sec. 208 (a)
5. New York News: October 25, 1964
6. New York Times: November 11, 1964
7. U. S. News and World Report: November 23, 1964
8. Congressional Record: July 21, 1965, p. 16985
9. ibid.

10. ibid.

11. New York Times: August 24, 1964

12. U. S. News and World Report: November 23, 1964

13. New York News: November 10, 1964

14. New York Times: August 19, 1964
    Alan Stang: *It's Very Simple*, Western Islands, Boston & Los Angeles, 1965, p. 173

15. National Review: September 15, 1964
    Alan Stang; *It's Very Simple*, Western Islands, Boston and Los Angeles, 1965, p. 171

16. New York Times: November 10, 1964
    Alan Stang: *It's Very Simple*, Western Islands, Boston and Los Angeles, 1965, p. 176

17. Anaheim Bulletin: April 19, 1965

18. ibid.

19. Fulton Lewis, Jr.: Los Angeles Herald Examiner, July 1, 1965

20. UPI release: Los Angeles Times, January 9, 1966

21. Congressional Record: August 18, 1965, p. 20086 and p. 20091

22. ibid.

23. ibid.

24. Congressional Record: August 16, 1965, pp. 19800-19802
    Rowland Evans & Robert Novak: Los Angeles Times, August 17, 1965

25. ibid.

26. Congressional Record: July 22, 1965, p. 17286
    Fulton Lewis, Jr.: Los Angeles Herald Examiner, June 29, 1965

27. Congressional Record: July 22, 1965, p. 17281

28. Congressional Record: July 22, 1965, p. 17286

29. Los Angeles Times: December 30, 1965

30. William F. Buckley, Jr.: Los Angeles Times, October 20, 1965

31. William F. Buckley, Jr.: Los Angeles Times, October 20, 1965

32. ibid.

33. ibid.

34. New York Times: August 27, 1964

35. Robert S. Allen & Paul Scott: December, 1964

36. Los Angeles Times: February 27, 1966

37. Civil Riots USA: Constructive Action, Inc, 1965

38. Look: July 28, 1964, p. 29

39. Look: July 28, 1964, p. 30

40. Drew Pearson: Los Angeles Times, October 8, 1965

41. U. S. News and World Report: October 18, 1965

42. AP release: Los Angeles Times, December 1, 1965

43. Fulton Lewis, Jr.: Los Angeles Herald Examiner, November 1, 1965

44. The New Yorker: December 26, 1964, p. 50

45. Fulton Lewis, Jr.: Los Angeles Herald Examiner, November 1, 1965

46. AP release: Los Angeles Times, December 1, 1965

Chapter 4:

1. Congressional Record: July 20, 1965, p. 16908
2. Los Angeles Times: May 26, 1965
3. Congressional Record: July 20, 1965, p. 16851
4. Los Angeles Times: January 5, 1966
5. TAXACTION, Inc., Altadena, California
6. Pasadena Star News: January 5, 1966
7. UPI release: Los Angeles Times, October 2, 1965
8. AP release: Pasadena Star News, October 3, 1965
9. ibid.
10. UPI release: Los Angeles Times, October 6, 1965
11. ibid.
12. The Wall Street Journal: January 18, 1965
13. Los Angeles Times: November 21, 1965

Chapter 5:

1. Northwest Pasadena Young Adult Project as submitted to the Pasadena Commission on Human Needs and Opportunities, p. 11 (Group Work Funds)
2. Los Angeles Herald Examiner: November 16, 1965
3. "Status Report on the Economic Opportunity Act of 1964 in the Los Angeles Area": Chief Administrative Officer (L. S. Hollinger) to the Los Angeles County Board of Supervisors, July 8, 1965
4. Congressional Record: August 18, 1965, p. 20090
5. Wall Street Journal: June 9, 1965
6. Russel Kirk: Los Angeles Times, August 3, 1965
7. Los Angeles Times: January 30, 1966
8. "Mobilizing Community Resources in a Dynamic Vocational Rehabilitation Project to Overcome Physical and Mental Disabilities that Cause or Magnify Poverty" as submitted by the Pasadena office of the California Department of Vocational Rehabilitation, March 19, 1965
9. Pasadena City College's Adult Education program as approved by the Office of Economic Opportunity through Stanley Sworder, Bureau of Adult Education, Sacramento, California
10. Pasadena Community Playhouse project proposal as submitted to the Economic and Youth Opportunities Agency (EYOA), August, 1965
11. Congressional Record: August 19, 1965, p. 20361
12. ibid.
13. Congressional Record: August 19, 1965, p. 20362
14. Los Angeles Times: November 19, 1965
15. Los Angeles Times: September 22, 1965 and September 23, 1965

16. The Northwest Pasadena Young Adult Project as submitted to the Pasadena Commission on Human Needs and Opportunities, p. 5
17. ibid. p. 11
18. ibid. p. 3
19. Los Angeles Times: November 4, 1965
20. ibid.
21. State of California: April 4, 1951 Legal Opinion on Labor Code, Sec. 1051; Penal Code 3107; Penal Code 11105; Attorney General's Opinion, July 1, 1960

Chapter 6:

1. Los Angeles Daily Journal: September 9, 1965
2. Pasadena Star News: August 10, 1965
3. Pasadena Star News: August 17, 1965 and July 22, 1965
4. Robert S. Allen & Paul Scott: Human Events, November 13, 1965
5. Los Angeles Daily Journal: September 9, 1965
6. Robert S. Allen & Paul Scott: Human Events, November 13, 1965
7. ibid.

Chapter 7:

1. Congressional Record: July 21, 1965, pp. 16977-8
2. Congressional Record: July 21, 1965, p. 16968
3. UPI release: Los Angeles Times, June 26, 1965
4. Congressional Record: July 20, 1965 p. 16873
5. Congressional Record: August 17, 1965, p. 19884
6. Congressional Record: July 22, 1965, p. 17290
7. Information Services Department, Economic and Youth Opportunities Agency (EYOA), Los Angeles, September 8, 1965
8. Pacific Oaks College: "Three Centers Project" as approved by the Office of Economic Opportunity (Washington), Fall, 1965. Copy on file at the Economic and Youth Opportunities Agency (EYOA), Los Angeles
9. Barry Goldwater: Los Angeles Times, September 17, 1965
10. Drew Pearson: Los Angeles Times, October 8, 1965
11. Congressional Record: July 21, 1965, p. 16991
12. Congressional Hearing (Ad-hoc subcommittee of the House Committee on Education and Labor): Will Rogers Park, Watts, California, August 7, 1965
13. Los Angeles Times: August 4, 1965
14. Congressional Record, July 21, 1965, p. 16992
15. ibid.
16. Los Angeles Times: August 22, 1965
17. Pasadena Star News: June 30, 1965 and July 2, 1965
18. California Federation of Pediatric Societies News: October 15, 1965 (Los Altos, California)
19. Congressional Record: July 21, 1965, p. 16992

20. Fulton Lewis, Jr.: Los Angeles Herald Examiner, November 16, 1965
21. U. S. News and World Report: November 15, 1965
22. ibid.
23. UPI release: Los Angeles Times, September 1, 1965

Chapter 8:

1. Los Angeles Times: July 30, 1965
   Pasadena Star News: October 19, 1965
   Santa Monica Evening Outlook: September 29, 1965
2. Los Angeles Times: July 7, 1965
3. Los Angeles Times: August 2, 1965
4. Santa Monica Evening Outlook: September 20, 1965
5. Los Angeles Times: October 14, 1965
6. Los Angeles Times: October 17, 1965
7. Los Angeles Times: February 26, 1966
8. Los Felez Tribune: October 28, 1965
9. Los Angeles Times: October 10, 1965 and October 19, 1965
10. Notes taken at the October 25, 1965 board meeting of the Economic and Youth Opportunities Agency (EYOA), Los Angeles
11. ibid.
12. ibid.

Chapter 9:

1. Charles Bartlett: Los Angeles Times, July 20, 1965
2. Congressional Presentation, Office of Economic Opportunity, April, 1965
3. Congressional Record: August 16, 1965, p. 19799, and August 17, 1965, p. 19881
4. Economic Opportunity Act (Public Law 88-452): Title 1, Part A, Sec. 105 (a)
5. Economic Opportunity Act (Public Law 88-452): Title 1, Part A, Sec. 105 (b)
6. UPI release: Los Angeles Times, January 7, 1966
7. Congressional Record: July 20, 1965, p. 16884
8. Congressional Record: August 16, 1965, p. 19807
9. Wall Street Journal: January 18, 1965
10. UPI release: Pasadena Star News, June 11, 1965
11. UPI release: Los Angeles Times, July 21, 1965
12. Fulton Lewis, Jr.: Los Angeles Herald Examiner, July 24, 1965
13. Congressional Record: July 20, 1965, p. 16877 and July 21, 1965, pp. 16961-2
14. AP release: Pasadena Star News, August 20, 1965 and August 22, 1965
15. Washington Post: Los Angeles Times, November 13, 1965
16. Los Angeles Herald Examiner: November 13, 1965
17. Human Events: February 26, 1966

18. Omaha Evening World Herald: Human Events, December 4, 1965
19. Fulton Lewis, Jr.: Los Angeles Herald Examiner, November 16, 1965
20. Life Line: "Job Corps," February 2, 1966 #33
21. Fulton Lewis, Jr.: Los Angeles Herald Examiner, October 14, 1965
22. New York Herald Tribune: December 11, 1965
23. Congressional Record: August 18, 1965, pp. 20090-1
24. *The Reporter*: March 25, 1965, p. 22
25. *The Reporter*: March 25, 1965, p. 21
26. Ruth Montgomery: Los Angeles Herald Examiner, September 13, 1965
27. Los Angeles Times: April 27, 1965
28. Photostat copy of Office of Economic Opportunity voucher used as payment for dinners in Pasadena, California
29. Human Events: February 12, 1966, p. 4
30. Charles Bartlett: Los Angeles Times, December 3, 1965
31. Congressional Record: August 16, 1965, p. 19799

Chapter 10:

1. Congressional Presentation

2. Economic Opportunity Act (Public Law 88-452): Title 1, Part B, Sec. 111, p. 5 and Title I, Part C. Sec. 121, p. 6
3. Economic Opportunity Act (Public Law 88-452): Title 1, Part B, Sec. 113 (a) (5), p. 5
4. Economic Opportunity Act (Public Law 88-542): Title 1, Part B, Sec. 113 (a) (4), p. 5
5. The Wall Street Journal: January 18, 1965
6. AP release: Los Angeles Times, January 20, 1965
7. Congressional Record: August 16, 1965, p. 19803
8. Fulton Lewis, Jr.: Los Angeles Herald Examiner, November 15, 1965
9. Fulton Lewis, Jr.: Los Angeles Herald Examiner, July 24, 1965
10. Los Angeles Times: August 2, 1965
11. Pasadena Independent: June 21, 1965
12. Pasadena Star News: January 20, 1965
13. Pasadena Star News: January 9, 1966
14. Pasadena Star News: October 24, 1965 and October 25, 1965
15. Los Angeles Times: July 21, 1965 and August 12, 1965
16. Congressional Record: August 19, 1965, p. 20343
    The Daily Californian: December 8, 1965
17. Berkeley Gazette: October 5, 1965
    Oakland Tribune: November 17, 1965
18. *Tocsin:* June 3, 1965, pp 1 and 4 (Oakland, California)
19. University of California Work-Study adjustment sheet #2, Spring, 1966
20. University of California Work-Study adjustment sheet #2, Spring, 1966

21. *Tocsin*: December 30, 1965
Oakland Tribune: November 17, 1965

22. University of California Work-Study adjustment sheet #2, Spring, 1966

23. Berkeley Gazette: October 5, 1965
Daily Californian: March 8, 1965 and December 12, 1963

24. UPI release: Los Angeles Times, October 30, 1965

25. Fulton Lewis, Jr.: Los Angeles Herald Examiner, November 15, 1965

26. Los Angeles Times: December 7, 1965

27. Pasadena Star News, January 5, 1965

28. New York Herald Tribune: September 5, 1965

29. New York Herald Tribune: September 5, 1965

30. Riverside Press: December, 1965

31. Fulton Lewis, Jr.: Los Angeles Herald Examiner, September 23, 1965

Chapter 11:

1. Congressional Record: July 20, 1965, p. 16873

2. Congressional Record: July 21, 1965, p. 16958

3. Congressional Record: July 20, 1965 (House of Representatives)

4. Congressional Record: July 21, 1965, p. 16972

5. Congressional Record: July 21, 1965, p. 16965

6. Congressional Record: July 20, 1965, p. 16873

7. ibid.

8. Congressional Record: July 20, 1965 and July 21, 1965 (House of Representatives)

9. Congressional Record: July 21, 1965, p. 16965

10. Richmond News Leader: Human Events, November 28, 1964

11. Congressional Record: July 20, 1965, p. 16862

12. Congressional Record: July 22, 1965, p. 17312

13. Congressional Record: July 21, 1965, p. 16953

14. Letter dated October 8, 1965: Los Angeles City School District, Gordon P. Trigg, Coordinator of Youth Opportunities

15. Los Angeles Youth Opportunities Board (later to become EYOA): "Funded Programs" (no date), received August, 1965

16. Pasadena Star News: April 21, 1965
Los Angeles Times: April 20, 1965

17. "Status Report on the Economic Opportunity Act of 1964 in the Los Angeles Area": Chief Administrative Officer (L. S. Hollinger), July 8, 1965

18. U. S. News and World Report: October 18, 1965

19. The Boston Traveler: November 18, 1965
The Boston Traveler: November 19, 1965 and November 30, 1965

20. Human Events: December 4, 1965

21. John Buckley (staff member of the subcommittee investigating task force of the House Committee on Education and Labor): January, 1966
22. Los Angeles Times: December 10, 1965
23. *The Reporter:* June 3, 1965, p. 22

Chapter 12:

1. "Status Report on the Economic Opportunity Act of 1964 in the Los Angeles Area": Chief Administrative Officer (L. S. Hollinger), July 8, 1965
2. Los Angeles Herald Examiner: July 20, 1965 and August 8, 1965
3. Los Angeles Times: July 14, 1965
4. Los Angeles Times: August 19, 1965
5. *Time:* August 20, 1965, p. 17
6. ibid.
7. Los Angeles Times: July 14, 1965
8. Los Angeles Times: January 12, 1966
9. Congressional Record: August 19, 1965, p. 20332
10. Los Angeles Times: August 6, 1965
11. Los Angeles Times: August 4, 1965
12. Los Angeles Times: July 10, 1965
13. Los Angeles Times: July 27, 1965
14. Los Angeles Times: August 11, 1965
15. Los Angeles Herald Examiner: August 7, 1965
16. People's World, September 14, 1965, p. 4
17. Los Angeles Times: August 8, 1965
18. John S. Gibson, Jr. (Los Angeles Councilman, 15th District): "Watts Area Improvements Since 1951," September 16, 1965, p. 16
19. ibid. pp. 11-12
20. Ruth Montgomery: Los Angeles Herald Examiner, September 6, 1965

Chapter 13:

1. The McCone Report: "Violence in the City—An End or a Beginning," December 2, 1965, pp. 23-24
2. ibid. p. 3
3. ibid.
4. Larry Hall: Los Angeles Times, August 15, 1965
5. The McCone Report: "Violence in the City—An End or a Beginning," December 2, 1965, p. 22
6. George S. Schuyler: Written for the North American Newspaper Alliance Inc., copyright, 1965
7. Los Angeles Times: December 8, 1965 and December 7, 1965
8. "Report of Joint Fact-Finding Committee on Un-American Activities," California Senate, Sacramento, 1947, p. 96: Reprint from "Civil Riots, USA," Constructive Action, Inc., 1965

9. ibid. pp. 70 & 78

10. ibid. p.170

11. ibid. 1947 & 1948

12. ibid.

13. Los Angeles Times: August 15, 1965

14. The McCone Report: "Violence in the City—An End or a Beginning," December 2, 1965, p.170

15. Los Angeles Times: September 14, 1965 and September 15, 1965

16. Los Angeles Times: August 17, 1965 and August 16, 1965

17. Los Angeles Times: August 25, 1965

18. Pasadena Star News: October 7, 1965

19. Los Angeles Times: November 27, 1965

20. Verified through personnel file at the Los Angeles Economic and Youth Opportunities Agency (EYOA), January, 1966

21. Santa Monica Evening Outlook: June 30, 1964 and July 23, 1964

22. *UCLA Bruin*: "Campus Roundup," May 17, 1963

23. "The Fire this Time, the W. E. DuBois Clubs' View of the Explosion in South Los Angeles": A salesman in the Progressive Book Store (Los Angeles) said, "This is the finest work written about the Watts riots," January, 1966

24. *UCLA Bruin*: "Campus Roundup," May 17, 1963

25. Fire and Police Research Association of Los Angeles (FiPo)

26. Richard Price and Bob Stewart: "Watts Action Committee and the Liberator," December, 1965, p. 1

27. Los Angeles Times: August 18, 1965

28. Pasadena Star News: August 19, 1965

29. Los Angeles Times: August 25, 1965

30. Pasadena Star News: September 17, 1965

31. Los Angeles Times: August 14, 1965 and August 24, 1965

32. Los Angeles Times: September 29, 1965

33. Los Angeles Times: August 14, 15, 1965

34. "Police Chief William H. Parker Speaks" prepared by the Community Relations Conference of Southern California, 2400 S. Western Ave, Los Angeles, Fall, 1965

35. Los Angeles Times: August 19, 1965 and August 20, 1965

36. Pasadena Star News: October 22, 1965

37. Los Angeles Times: August 21, 1965

38. The McCone Report: "Violence in the City—An End or a Beginning," December 2, 1965, p. 88

39. Los Angeles Times: August 21, 1965

40. ibid.

41. Los Angeles Times: August 27, 1965

42. ibid.

43. Los Angeles Times: September 21, 1965

Fire and Police Research Association of Los Angeles (FiPo): July, 1964, and August, 1964

Los Angeles Times: August 14, 1965 and August 19, 1965

Chapter 14:

1. Edward Howden, Chief of the California State Division of Fair Employment Practices (FEPC): Los Angeles Times, November 24, 1965
2. Los Angeles Times: August 17, 1965
3. Los Angeles Times: September 2, 1965
4. Los Angeles Times: August 31, 1965
5. Los Angeles Times: August 18, 1965
6. Los Angeles Times: August 18, 1965

Chapter 15:

1. Los Angeles Herald Examiner: August 19, 1965
2. ibid.
3. Los Angeles Times: September 3, 1965
4. ibid.
5. Los Angeles Herald Examiner: September 9, 1965
6. Los Angeles Times: October 3, 1965 and December 30, 1965
7. Los Angeles Times: October 5, 1965
8. Los Angeles Herald Examiner: October 6, 1965
9. AP release: Pasadena Star News: October 11, 1965
10. Los Angeles Herald Examiner: October 6, 1965
11. AP release: Pasadena Star News: October 13, 1965
12. Los Angeles Herald Examiner: October 21, 1965
13. Los Angeles Herald Examiner: October 28, 1965
14. Los Angeles Herald Examiner: November 1, 1965
15. Los Angeles Herald Examiner: November 10, 1965
16. Los Angeles Herald Examiner: November 5, 1965
17. Los Angeles Times: November 16, 1965
18. Los Angeles Times: November 19, 1965
19. Los Angeles Herald Examiner: November 25, 1965
20. Los Angeles Herald Examiner: November 30, 1965
21. Pasadena Star News: December 13, 1965
22. Los Angeles Times: December 15, 1965
23. Los Angeles Times: December 16, 1965
24. Los Angeles Times: January 30, 1966
25. Los Angeles Times: November 23, 1965 and February 27, 1966
26. Los Angeles Times: January 4, 1966 and February 2, 1966
27. AP release: Los Angeles Times, January 7, 1966
28. Los Angeles Times: January 11, 1966
29. Los Angeles Herald Examiner: December 10, 1965
30. Pasadena Star News: September 8, 1965
31. Los Angeles Times: October 21, 1965
32. Los Angeles Times: January 30, 1966
33. United Way, Inc.: Letter dated July 16, 1965 from Daniel H. Ridder, President, United Way, Inc. to Mrs. Ralph W. Newman
34. Los Angeles Times: April 11, 1965
35. Notes taken at the Economic and Youth Opportunities

Agency (EYOA) board meeting, October 18, 1965 (Los Angeles)

36. Notes taken at the Economic and Youth Opportunities Agency (EYOA) board meeting October 4, 1965 (Los Angeles).

37. Los Angeles Herald Examiner: October 11, 1965

38. Los Angeles Herald Examiner: November 30, 1965 and December 2, 1965

39. Pasadena Star News: February 14, 1966

40. Los Angeles Times, March 1, 1966

41. Casper Weinberger: Los Angeles Times, September 1, 1965

42. Los Angeles Herald Examiner: Editorial, August 8, 1965

42. Los Angeles Times: March 3, 1966

43. EYOA Public Information Officer, William Rivera on the George Putman KTLA news, March 2, 1966

44. Los Angeles Times: September 20, 1965

45. George Jordan: "Seasoning the News," Orange County Republican, January, 1966

46. Los Angeles Times: December 27, 1965

47. Rowland Evans and Robert Novak: Los Angeles Times, January 13, 1966

48. Pasadena Star News: August 26, 1965

49. Congressional Record: August 19, 1965, p. 20372

50. Los Angeles Times: August 17, 1965

51. Los Angeles Times: August 30, 1965

52. UPI release: Los Angeles Herald Examiner, November 17, 1965

Los Angeles Times: November 21, 1965

INDEX

HELP

INFORM

OTHERS!

GIVE
"PASS THE POVERTY PLEASE"

To friends, relatives, neighbors and community leaders.

Thousands of copies are being distributed in every part of the United States, in churches, offices, factories, clubs, trade associations and labor unions.

Do your part in this vital educational job. Order copies of "Pass The Poverty Please" for your own use, at the low quantity prices listed below.

Quantity Prices

1 copy	$ .75	10 copies	$ 5	100 copies	$ 30
3 copies	$2.00	25 copies	$10	500 copies	$125

1,000 or more copies $.20 each
Lower prices on quantities of 5,000 or more

Order from: CONSTRUCTIVE ACTION INC.
P.O. Box 4006
Whittier, California 90607
Telephone: Area Code 213-693-0764